Scott James has a hands-on, deeply philosophical, understanding of the world we live in and of the need to address the issues that will impact his children and mine—all the children of our planet. This book guides us along a pathway to truly understand the nature of our collective futures. It is a brilliant tapestry that interweaves the emergency preparedness and sustainability movements.

John Perkins
New York Times Bestselling Author

Scott James' book, *Prepared Neighborhoods*, will save lives. It is must-read, page-turner despite its daunting subject matter, and Scott's ability to transform a scary future into a manageable and more enjoyable present is visionary. As part of our extensive earthquake preparedness coverage at KING5 in Seattle, Scott's expertise has proved invaluable. He has the rare skill of being able to speak comfortably with both experts and layman, decoding science and psychology into the manageable sound bites.

Steve Bunin
NBC Emmy Award Winning News Anchor

Books like Scott's are resilience stabilizers, helping us navigate the circuitous path of change. Communities come together for solutions. Going it alone is a myth; the more we embrace our collective wisdom and skills, the stronger and more resilient our communities become. Oh, and make sure that those communities are building fun into the mix – no one wants a future unless it is going to be fun!

David Johnson
Advisor, Transition Towns US

Scott James has filled a missing link in the transition to a new economy. The neighborhood unit – bigger than a household and smaller than a city – is the essential human scale for building community resilience and preparedness. Get your neighbors together to read Prepared Neighborhoods and act!

Chuck Collins
Senior Scholar, Institute for Policy Studies
Co-Founder, Resilience Circles Network

Prepared Neighborhoods is a powerful resource for both small communities and individual households. Scott James clearly lays out the "What Ifs" many of us harbor in the backs of our minds and proposes sustainable and resilient ways to address them. Best of all, this book is written for real neighborhoods, using the language they speak in and clear examples.

Caitria O'Neill
Founder, Recovers

This is a beautifully written, essential book for our times. So inspiring...this idea of connecting neighbor to neighbor to help and more fully enjoy each other. Prepared Neighborhoods gives us practical advice and real world examples about how to create a resilient neighborhood, leading to deeper connections and true peace of mind!

Kimberly Gallagher, M.Ed.
Author of the Herb Fairies Series
Creator of Wildcraft! An Herbal Adventure
Game

This book's impressive coverage of preparedness is both wide-ranging and deep. The organization and writing style of this information-rich book make it particularly easy to read. It is clear and understandable. Small steps to ease into each category of preparedness are highlighted. The content can be generalized to most regions and settings from rural countryside to densely populated cities. Important nuggets of information abound in Prepared Neighborhoods!

Leslie Marshall RN, PhD
Professor Emerita
University of Iowa College of Nursing

With the help of a resilient community—interwoven with networks of self-reliant and prepared friends and neighbors—we stand a much better chance for not just surviving, but actually thriving after a long term catastrophe. How to build such a network and community? Scott James has thought long and hard on this subject. He and his neighbors and friends are not just thinking about it, they are doing it, and they are sharing their practical knowhow through his excellent new book.

Do yourself, your family, your friends, and your neighbors a favor—buy this book and take the time to start building resilience and preparedness into your neighborhood. Do it now, while there is still time for a relaxed leisurely approach, and let Scott's very readable book guide you through the process. Highly recommended!

— Matthew Stein: Author of "When Technology Fails: A Manual for Self-Reliance, Sustainability & Surviving the Long Emergency" and "When Disaster Strikes: A Comprehensive Guide to Emergency Planning and Crisis Survival"

PREPARED
NEIGHBORHOODS

Creating Resilience
One Street at a Time

SCOTT JAMES

Copyright © 2017 by Scott James

HOLD
FAST

Hold Fast Publishing

ISBN 978-0-692-85168-5
ISBN 978-0-692-85169-2 (ebook)
Printed in the United States of America
Library of Congress Cataloging-in-Publication:
2018905781–Third Edition–

Senior Editor: LuAn K. Johnson, PhD
Editor: Robin Dorfman
Art Direction: Chris McMasters
Cover Design: Alexander Vulchev
Typesetting: Mariam Samani
Illustrations: Paul Kearsley

DEDICATION

To Justice and Mercy, our hope for the future.

Scott James

To the thousands of neighborhoods it has been my pleasure, personally, to help prepare, I thank you. You have taught me that prepared individuals, families, and neighborhoods are the foundation of resilient communities. Your willing support to one another as neighbors, especially during a time of actual disasters, gives me great hope for our collective future.

LuAn K. Johnson, PhD

A portion of the author's royalties are donated to preparedness education.

CONTENTS

HI NEIGHBOR!.

SHARING MEALS.

MAP YOUR NEIGHBORHOOD.

BUILDING SOCIAL RESILIENCE

"We must rebuild functioning communities with closer ties to the land not just in nostalgic fantasy, not just in token preservation, but in substantial daily practice. We must reclaim the commons."

Brian Donohue
Associate Professor at Brandeis
University and author

Resilience is a worthwhile pursuit, but how do we build strength into our lives as citizens and into our towns as stakeholders? The answer lies within our neighborhoods. The neighborhood is where sustainability meets preparedness. It is one step beyond caring for your own loved ones, and one step back from where emergency professionals serve at the county, state, and national levels.

Our focus for this book is one of mutual aid among residents, not disaster relief provided by a government agency. We are not promoting going solo. Self-sufficiency for every citizen is not only unattainable, it is undesirable. Group resilience–neighbors taking care of neighbors–is the desired state of being.

As we learn from the Stoics, when rationally viewing disasters, or in anticipation of one, we can see the opportunities contained within. Opportunities for the greater community, deeper relationships, and corrected priorities.

We each decide what story to tell ourselves and others: one based on love, or one based on fear. Let's pursue the story of love, strength, and group resilience!

Imagine with me a group of neighbors—just like you might have—with whom we'll check in at the beginning of each chapter.

The house had been dark and cold for four days. No electricity, no heat, no running water and, now, no food.

Ross watched as his children ate through the last of their "Three Days, Three Ways" emergency kit rations, belatedly realizing this emergency was going to last much longer than just a weekend. He began to feel panic pushing into his normally clear-thinking mind. It bothered him that his children were drinking stale Coca-Colas found in the back of their garage for breakfast. But they had no drinking water and had already emptied the refrigerator and pantry.

No one was sure how long the power would be out. No one knew when the grocery stores would be restocked. No one knew when the gas stations would receive more fuel. No one knew when the bridge would be repaired nor when the roads would have their rubble, downed trees, and power lines removed. And with both cell phones and landlines not working, communication was at a standstill.

Lisa came downstairs and went straight to the front door.

"Where are you going?" Ross asked his wife, an edge in his voice. He realized he was sweating, despite the chill.

"To the neighbors," Lisa calmly replied as she added an outer layer to her sweater, long-sleeved shirt, and flannel-lined Carhartts. "The stores are empty and so is our pantry. If we're going to get through this, we'll need their help."

Our Journey

In the neighborhood we can focus on what is changeable and significant for surviving and recovering quickly from a wide-scale event, whether it is a short-term natural disaster (earthquake, fire, flood, even military action) or a long-term economically-induced emergency (our current situation where the global oil predicament, climate change, and other shocks to the system are having implications for how we will live in the decades ahead). The quest for community has never been stronger. And the recognition that all is not well is growing. We need a way to take action; action that can move us from a paralyzing fear to an activating hope. It can begin in our own homes, streets, and neighborhoods.

Neighbors taking care of neighbors with a bit of positive-focused foresight and planning can move us further along the sustainability continuum toward a more resilient and bright future. The resilience we so desperately need in our lives is best built not just from within, but also from our relationships with others. It is time to get to know our neighbors again, as those are the relationships we'll depend on most heavily during an emergency.

As Jay Walljasper proposes in his essay *Changing the World One Block at a Time,* "The neighborhood is the basic building block of human society, and practical efforts to save the planet start right there. Whether a rural village in India, a suburban subdivision in California, or a bohemian quarter in Berlin, neighborhoods shape people's lives in powerful and surprising ways." Walljasper's essay is just one of many excellent pieces in *Less is More* by Cecile Andrews and Wanda Urbanska. Walljasper's full essay is well worth a read, as is Dave Wann's piece about the "real wealth of neighborhoods."

Watching the great natural and economic emergencies of our time impact our country over the last few decades, my family has journeyed from a "blissfully-clueless" state through an "informed-enough-to-be-worried" state to arrive finally at the "act-now" state.

During our journey, I began to blog at OptOutEnMasse. com (borrowing a phrase from Joel Salatin) about our successes and failures with exurban homesteading experiments (exurban is the zoning classification between suburban and rural). Over the years, it became clear that true self-sufficiency was not only unattainable but also undesirable. In addition to opting out of the negative aspects of the American system as we know it, we also needed to opt in to something new, something positive, something local, and something that builds community.

We began to talk to others about emergencies beyond our own country as well. The Japanese tsunami. The Christchurch earthquake. The financial woes of the European Union. Brexit! Within our country, we looked at both Hurricane Katrina in 2005 and the Louisiana flooding in 2016. Worldwide, Munich Reinsurance Company reported that claims due to natural disasters reached a record $135 billion in 2017. The list goes on and on.

This emerging worldwide crisis presents an opportunity for us to look at who we are. Who we are as a species living on a fragile space station. Who we are as caring neighbors. Who we are as citizens. It's a conversation that is increasingly finding a wider and more mainstream audience. As Rebecca Solnit describes in her brilliant book, *A Paradise Built in Hell*, "The word *emergency* comes from *emerge*, to rise out of, the opposite of merge, which comes from *mergere*, to be within or under a liquid, immersed, submerged. An emergency is a separation from the familiar, a sudden emergence into a new atmosphere, one that often demands we ourselves rise to the occasion."

Learning from Our Elders

My grandfather maintained a significant victory garden until his death and had a wide variety of practical homesteading skills. Despite my father's Ph.D. and years of experience running organizations (quite successfully), my grandfather's hands-on knowledge simply did not transfer down to him. I notice many folks of his generation lack the practical experience to grow their own food or weather a two-week winter storm without electricity.

These are skills I learned myself in the last ten years from books, blogs, and buddies (plus a fair amount of trial and error... mostly error!). More than once, my father has remarked to me with a bit of humorous wonder in his voice how proud my grandfather would be of my efforts to develop self-reliance. And good news! We don't have to learn the practical skills (e.g. farming) of a previous generation by ourselves, but can learn collectively, in conjunction with our neighbors. In our journey, we've discovered individual self-reliance not to be the ultimate goal... community-reliance is much more valuable!

At the other end of the spectrum from individual/family preparedness is a huge amount of literature, only some of which is helpful to citizens like us. It is full of technical jargon—it assumes the audience is solely national/international emergency professionals—and primarily useful for large groups of people (like mass exoduses of refugees). It is difficult to scale down their concepts to the neighborhood level.

(A quick aside on my use of "citizens" throughout this book: I use it in the context of a person belonging to a specific community; it does not refer to legal citizenship of a specific country.)

Attitude Is Better Than Gear

True preparedness can only come from inside ourselves. We seek to create a solid, balanced platform within from which we can weather any disruptions or shocks. No amount of gear or even those crucial relationships with others will help unless we've looked deep into ourselves and decided that not only will we survive a major incident, but we also will recover quickly so we can help our family and neighbors.

I've long been a fan of the practical wisdom of lightweight backpacking guru Ray Jardine. His wisdom goes well beyond espousing minimalist gear to help you hike fast and far. I've not yet had the chance to spend time with him, but there is a particular passage from one of his books that is spot on. His metaphor of cooking a meal over a balanced tripod after a day of backpacking is apt for anyone seeking to change their mindset from one dominated by our consumer-focused culture to a more balanced perspective.

"The tripod standing over the cook-fire is sacred to me, in the sense that its three legs represent elements fundamental in us all; namely the physical, intellectual, and spiritual. More specifically, each leg corresponds to our awareness in that particular realm, and our ability to function in it.

In order for the cook-fire tripod to serve its purpose, each leg must be strong and capable. If one leg is weak, then the whole tripod lacks strength. But when equally developed, the three legs work together and make us exceptionally capable in all our pursuits."

Other thought leaders consider attitude to be paramount as well. Becky Lerner, author of the book *Dandelion Hunter: Foraging the Urban Wilderness,* spoke with me from her foraging grounds in Portland, Oregon, about the importance of moving from a "Lone Ranger" survivor perspective to a collaborative one that builds community.

Becky told me what she teaches others in her foraging classes. "Survival is a collective activity. The solo survivalist is a Western myth; ditch it now. The best insurance plan is an empowered community. Each of us has unique gifts, strengths, and abilities. Perhaps you are a great builder, your partner is an excellent cook, your friend is a talented clothes-maker, and your neighbor has a knack with medicinal plants. Maybe the person living around the corner has a basket-weaving hobby and makes clay pottery, and is truly outstanding at these things. The truly wise survivalist will acknowledge these inclinations and see the advantage of viewing survival as a collective endeavor."

Our Pacific Northwest neighbor, Portland, seems to have as many strong communities as Seattle, where I live. Becky and I compared notes on shared friends and contacts in sustainable communities and subcultures through the colorful neighborhoods enjoyed by each of our cities. Becky commented, "This is what we observe in successful, sustainable cultures. In hunter-gatherer societies, the community is essential; one goes out into the bush to try to survive alone only for special short-term purposes, such as vision quests and rites of passage. The experienced forager, too, can appreciate the efficiency of gathering acorns or blackberries with friends rather than alone. For most of us, it's hard to be a human Swiss army knife. I think that's why we're naturally inclined to be social."

I asked Becky about her thoughts for the future, particularly in the urban areas in which most of the world's population lives. She replied, "What will our future look like? It could begin with a block party and lead to a neighborhood coming together to create front lawn share-cropping, rooftop gardens, rainwater harvesting, and even wild backyard lawns. The possibilities are endless!"

The Neighborhood is the Key

The neighborhood is where we find the sweet spot for resilience. It consists of small groups of citizens bound by geography who are able to care for themselves during an emergency, whether it is a short-term natural disaster or a long-term economically induced emergency. For clarity, we'll use the term 'neighborhood' to define a collection of up to 20 families (on a street or in an apartment building) and 'community' for anything larger than that.

We must be able to care for ourselves without the aid of professionals during a short-term emergency because they are simply not coming (as they will also tell you). After a large natural disaster, the fire and police departments are required to do drive-by assessments of the entire damaged area before they are allowed to respond to the first house fire or victim. Yikes! In a wide-scale emergency like an earthquake, our professionals will be overwhelmed with acute situations; they will not be coming to check on you in your neighborhood. This is where mutual aid among residents is so important.

FEMA (Federal Emergency Management Agency) has made it clear that the government can't respond to historic devastation like Hurricane Harvey alone. The head of FEMA made repeated direct appeals via television after that disaster for widespread citizen engagement. And the United States is not alone in this request for full engagement for relief and recovery efforts from the population. In both Chile and Japan, public and private sectors worked together to restore most of their communication and electrical power in less than three weeks after getting slammed with 8.8 and 9.0 earthquakes.

In our country's economic reality, emergency response professionals find themselves underfunded, understaffed, and simply stretched too thin to provide care for residents on each street. We simply can't rely on city, state and federal planning, and must step back to individual and family level planning, and especially planning on the neighborhood level, where preparedness meets the sustainability movement.

It's up to us, citizens, to create more resilient neighborhoods, before the emergency hits. And we can!

Preparedness, Please Meet Sustainability

Emergency preparedness and sustainability are best interconnected at the neighborhood level. By beginning the conversation with emergency preparedness, positive social and environmental change is created for millions of Americans who normally shy away from any conversation about "the green movement."

Neighbors who would not normally engage in a conversation about the environment become deeply involved in emergency preparedness projects because they see the direct benefits for themselves. When you and your neighbors agree to check on each other after a natural disaster, you set the stage for future sustainability projects to succeed. Please note that neighbor relationships are the core building blocks of resilience for both a localized emergency, such a single tornado that affects one Oklahoman town, and a wide-scale natural disaster, such as an earthquake affecting Oregon, Washington, and British Columbia.

The ongoing experiment in our town (details at bainbridgeprepares.org) connects official disaster relief initiatives (often driven by city and county professionals) to the sustainability movement (often driven by citizen activists) with the support of the civic service sector (e.g. service organizations like Rotary International). It contributes to the conversation already happening in individual homesteads and at the federal level by adding community organizing around sustainability. These projects range from group purchases of emergency water supplies to pea patch gardens, all of which equip our neighborhoods to better survive and recover from future emergencies, be they short or long.

These interpersonal connections will be crucial to thriving in the coming "Long Emergency," as author and social critic James Kunstler has aptly labeled what life will look like when oil becomes unaffordable. In numerous books and podcasts, Kunstler describes the negative effects on society of the continued (and misguided) expectation of inexpensive oil. Peak Oil will create scarcities affecting almost every aspect of our lives. This also references a preparedness mindset that is important to maintain even during non-emergency times.

While an earthquake or hurricane can create an immediate loss of your home, for many people who live paycheck to paycheck, so can the sudden loss of a job or hospitalization of a spouse. The same four weeks of food you set aside to survive after an earthquake can be the four weeks of food you use when a huge unexpected emergency room bill depletes your already tight budget for the month. Preparing for the Long Emergency builds resilience into your life for good times and bad.

We're seeing a groundswell of activity among civic and government groups from Portland, Oregon to Portland, Maine, building resilience into our systems. Countless families have begun shelter-in-place preparations in their homes for weathering a natural disaster; just do a quick online search for "urban homesteads." What is missing in many of those locations is the bridge between these two efforts, which is the neighborhood. And yet that is the point in scale at which we can see rapid progress being made. This is not a new concept; you can read about hundreds of years of group resilience in communities like the Amish, marveling at their ability to quickly rally around a single family or project and push it to completion. In recent decades, we've also seen how citizens dig in after a natural disaster to begin life again after the first responders (firefighters, police, EMTs) leave.

How to Rebuild a City by Gisleson, Thompson & Burke is an excellent short book that provides insights into how individual citizens, streets, and then entire neighborhoods in New Orleans took on the task of rebuilding their city after Hurricane Katrina when aid from state and federal sources was nonexistent. Rather than a coordinated state or federal government effort, it was a patchwork of smaller but significant efforts by a wide variety of individuals and small groups rallying Amish-style around specific projects.

In the wake of the New Orleans tragedy, the authors document the natural progression of emergency preparedness (and direct response, in this case) to sustainable engagement and reconstruction. As the citizens rebuilt their city, they found an opportunity to rework civic systems into versions that better matched their ideals of social justice and environmental stewardship.

Much of the work was citizen-led, street by street, one neighborhood at a time. For instance, immediately after Katrina the volunteer-run New Orleans Food & Farm Network organized teams of citizens to create localized food maps so citizens could locate sources of food within walking distance, one street at a time.

In the years after the disaster, the organization grew rapidly, spurring other food-related citizen organizations that have been reclaiming abandoned lots for community food gardens. These are everyday citizens working to increase their city's food security, one urban lot at a time. Via broad public interest, the city is also learning about healthy eating, sustainability practices, and group resilience.

Responsible Citizens

During a wide-scale incident like an earthquake, fire and police departments and county emergency planning departments will be focused on primary infrastructure, not individual citizens. Our professionals will eventually restore our basic infrastructure, but in the short term, they will focus only on the most acute needs of our community.

In the meantime, citizens can take responsibility for the majority of our population's welfare at the level of their individual neighborhoods. Citizens acting in small teams can help a neighborhood recover quickly from an incident. Food can be shared. Fires can be avoided by turning off a neighbor's natural gas.

I am lucky enough to live on Bainbridge Island near Seattle, home to several leading organizations in the sustainability community such as YES! Magazine and nature-based education pioneer Islandwood. The island contains a larger-than-normal percentage of deep thinkers and writers on the topic of resilience, such as David Korten and John Perkins. And we have a citizen-led organization called 'Sustainable Bainbridge' that shepherds activist groups working on issues ranging from clean watersheds to local food to alternative transportation.

It was within Sustainable Bainbridge that I first launched the idea of a citizen-led preparedness organization, recognizing that the combination of emergency preparedness with the sustainability movement can build some much-needed resilience into our lives. Many towns both large and small have similar organizations, usually with either "Transition" or "Sustainable" in their names. These groups are citizen-led, affinity-based, and community-focused, making them natural funnels for the introduction of neighborhood emergency preparation strategies.

One of the best is Dr. LuAn Johnson's Map Your Neighborhood (MYN), a cleverly designed flip chart available from the Washington State Emergency Management website as well as through many local fire departments. The MYN process prepares your small group of immediate neighbors to move through nine steps together in the case of an emergency. Even with the slow and inadequate response from state and federal teams during Hurricane Katrina, if groups of citizens in neighborhoods across Louisiana and the surrounding states had organized around a program like MYN, they could have mitigated much of the tragedy we witnessed.

The success of MYN lies in its recognition of the importance of relationships. Creating a prepared neighborhood is more than remembering, "Stephen has a chainsaw I can borrow should that large tree fall across our driveway." It's more than a casual conversation with a neighbor about when to evacuate for the latest hurricane bearing down on your town.

A prepared neighborhood is an interconnected set of relationships that you can depend on during an immediate crisis as well as a "long emergency."

Those relationships will produce more well-being for you and your loved ones than any amount of supplies you have in storage, and will have many positive side benefits during non-emergency times as well.

While older texts recommend three days' worth of emergency food and water be kept on hand, many federal and state emergency planning departments now recommend at least 14 days. Several excellent books that I'll mention throughout this book offer practical steps that can be taken to gather and store these recommended supplies to prepare your home and your family for emergencies. ThePrepared. com—the "new kid on the block" in prepper websites— offers a number of useful guides and checklists. I've come to think of ThePrepared.com as the Consumer Reports of the preparedness world with extensively researched and documented articles (calling them blog posts doesn't really do them justice; they are more like lengthy magazine-style articles).

But even one year's worth of stored food will dwindle to a few weeks' supply when the rest of your neighborhood arrives at your doorstep in need. And the water your family has stored properly will be exhausted in a matter of days when sharing with friends and extended family.

Is the answer to hoard your supplies and force your neighbors away at gunpoint? Of course not! The most patriotic and loving response we can have in a time of crisis is generosity. And that starts with your immediate neighbors.

In a prepared neighborhood, your resources won't be exhausted by your generosity to your neighbors. That's because, in a prepared neighborhood, the resilience created by following principles of sustainability will ensure that systems will remain in place and that stores for everyone will last much longer than three days, two weeks, or even a year.

Mapping Your Neighborhood

Due to the transitory nature of American urban and suburban areas, few citizens have strong direct neighbor connections. But direct connections are still possible in this age of social media. Whether you begin by "friending" your neighbor online or simply by using the old-fashioned method of knocking on their front door, introducing yourself to just one other neighbor is the best way to start.

Find someone close enough that you could run to their place to borrow a cup of honey; that is the same distance you'll go in an emergency to ask for help. Then repeat the process a few more times, encouraging that first connection to do the same, and in no time you'll at least have a friendly "wave to each other" relationship with your immediate neighbors.

These face-to-face relationships help to re-localize our communities. "Re-localization" means bringing back much of what was outsourced, especially relationships. Facebook friends will not be there physically in a crisis to help you, but technology can still play a supporting role. An encouraging new wave of smartphone applications and websites are focused on creating and connecting neighbors at the hyper-local level.

British anthropologist Robin Dunbar coined the term "Rule of 150," defined as the "suggested cognitive limit to the number of people with whom one can maintain stable social relationships and thus numbers larger than this generally require more restrictive rules, laws, and enforced norms to maintain a stable, cohesive group." When a group grows to over 150 individuals, cohesion loosens and hierarchy begins to hinder communication. The example I learned about in MBA school was the company Gore Associates, an enormous company that manages to continue its growth and high employee satisfaction by applying the Rule of 150, limiting each of their buildings to no more than 150 employees. This same thinking can be applied to our group resilience projects at the neighborhood level.

Once you've initiated contact with at least one neighbor, you are ready to pursue the Map Your Neighborhood (MYN) program. The name may be slightly misleading for citizens in larger neighborhoods as they will really be mapping only their two to twenty immediate neighbors rather than an entire neighborhood.

Dr. Johnson's nine-step program is a straightforward and friendly way to gain neighborhood commitment for mutual care, from watching over children and the elderly to preventing fires by shutting off gas tanks to staying comfortable in the seasonal elements.

These are the nine steps in the MYN program that should be done immediately following a disaster.

At home:

Step 1. Take care of your loved ones.

Step 2. Dress for safety. A bicycle helmet or hardhat protects from falling debris. Sturdy shoes protect from broken glass. Leather gloves protect from sharp objects.

Step 3. Check the natural gas or propane at your home. Shut off if necessary. This is one of the best ways to prevent fire.

Step 4. Shut off water at the house main to trap water in your home. This will keep pollutants out of possible drinking water, like that in your water heater.

Step 5. Place a Help or OK sign on your front door or window. Posting the sign helps your neighbors locate those who need help first.

Step 6. Put your fire extinguisher on the sidewalk or where neighbors can see it. This way, if a neighbor has a small fire after a disaster, extinguishers are on hand.

With your neighbors:

Step 7. After steps 1-6 are completed, go to the Neighborhood Gathering Site.

Step 8. Form teams at the Neighborhood Gathering Site:

1. Team 1 will listen to the Emergency Alert System (AM/FM radio), or to an NOAA Weather Radio and keep neighbors informed of what they learn.

2. Team 2 will check on neighbors who are elderly, those disabled, or homes where children may be alone.

3. Team 3 will check all natural gas meters and propane tanks, and shut off the gas as necessary.

4. Team 4 will check on all homes with the "Help" card displayed on the front door or window, or with no card showing. Be prepared to give first aid. Trust your instincts. If something feels unsafe, stay out.

Step 9. After your team has completed its work, go back to the Neighborhood Gathering Site. Share what you have done with the rest of your neighbors.

I've added a "Step 10" to Dr. Johnson's list to bridge the gap from a single street to the larger community and region through our shared sense of civic duty.

Step 10: Designate a hub location staffed by trained volunteers under the guidance of emergency professionals that is within walking distance of your neighborhood. This will be a natural gathering point where folks would go for news, medical supplies, emotional relief, food, water, and weather relief.

We'll talk more about this hub concept in the shelter chapter, but Step 10 goes beyond just this physical location. It also involves sharing your unique skills and expertise with others, via that neighborhood shelter or elsewhere in your community, after a wide-scale disaster.

There are some special considerations for the MYN program should you live in an apartment or condominium. Using the same principle of 2-20 homes per MYN group, organize yourself by floors if possible to avoid extra climbing of stairs (remember no electricity means no elevator). Each building will also need an overall MYN Captain to coordinate each individual group.

In addition to a Neighborhood Gathering Site outside the building, each floor should have a Floor Coordination Site on each floor of the building where residents report after completing steps 1-6.

Regardless of the type of home, here's an example of the benefits of Dr. Johnson's program: One MYN street may have three medically trained citizens living on it and another MYN street may have two structural engineers. When an emergency such as earthquake strikes, after each MYN street has ensured its initial stability, residents can begin to communicate with other nearby streets to assess their needs. Being able to swap a nurse for a structural engineer greatly benefits both locations.

A silver lining to the dramatic increase in the number of recent natural disasters is the opportunity to talk about preparedness with our neighbors. These MYN conversations—while serious and based on real, dire emergencies—can also be made fun and interesting.

We've found a seasonal party (for instance, celebrating winter holidays) to be a great mechanism for gathering neighbors to discuss MYN principles. They form the basis for deeper relationships, community-enhancing group projects, and more resilient homes and neighborhoods.

One of Dr. Johnson's steps in the MYN process is to list the tools and equipment you have that may be useful in an emergency. But there is no need for that list to be reserved only for times of emergencies.

Those tools can be used on a regular basis to create a more beautiful and attractive place to live; turning the vacant lot on your street into an urban vegetable garden; building an Amish-style barn-raising project for the widow in the condo unit next door; completing an earthquake-proofing weekend for your apartment complex; sweeping through homes in a conversation-filled party to bolt all heavy furniture to the walls; creating that shared rainwater harvesting system for your apartment building's rooftop garden.

Now imagine that you have an entire community organized under the MYN principles and the sustainability-related projects have begun. Neighbors are talking to neighbors more than they're talking to Facebook friends. Mobile apps on our smartphones are encouraging the gifting and barter of services and foodstuffs within our "walksheds" (the area within walking distance of our home). More time is being spent in our specific neighborhoods with less time spent running errands in our cars. We're well on our way to creating a more livable and vibrant town!

First Steps

The neighborhood is where we can build lasting resilience; it will be the focus of this conversation to help North American citizens move further along the sustainability continuum together, toward a more resilient (and bright!) future. At some point in the reading of these chapters, you may feel a sense of despair or find yourself feeling a bit overwhelmed. That would mean you are 100% normal!

Most of the projects we'll cover are simply a series of small, doable steps. Completing these quick actions will help you avoid or shed any feelings of guilt that may arise from not having tackled the larger topic of preparedness earlier. The fact that you are reading this book now is a significant first step towards becoming more prepared!

Moving your reality from Point A (where you are today) to Point B (where you want yourself, your neighborhood, and your community to be) can be a multi-year process that may seem daunting at first glance. But you've already taken the first step (reading this book) and are likely further down the preparedness road than you realize. It is important to recognize that it is never too late to start the preparedness projects that you'll read about in the coming chapters. Completing small projects from each chapter is a proven method to build quick successes that "snowball" into a significant positive change in your life as well as those around you.

To get started, consider this three-step process before you jump into the next chapter:

1. Have the intention to live a resilient life in a prepared neighborhood, making the creation of this life and neighborhood a priority in your life.

2. Carve out time in your busy schedule to begin daily/weekly work on this intention, starting with the completion of this book.

3. Make a public commitment to begin (or continue with renewed vigor) on this path. Studies show that a commitment made known to others—through email, social media, or verbally—has a significantly higher probability of being reached. When you reach that milestone, be sure to circle back with those same folks to whom you made the public commitment and celebrate it together! As you can see, we've got a lot of fun work to do with friends and neighbors. So let's get going!

Ready? Start!

When talking about resetting our culture and radically overhauling basic tenants of our society, it can be easy to feel overwhelmed. What happened to just setting aside some water and food for a winter storm? Let's take a step back from societal change to a scale we can move from discussion to action: the neighborhood.

Every once in a while, I feel overwhelmed by the negativity of it all or the endless lists of things for which I could be preparing my family and neighborhood. As you wrap up this book, you may be feeling the same way. When that happens, I pause, look at my relatively short, prioritized task list, take a deep breath, and move toward getting the next item checked off.

So if you are just starting out, here's your one task to do this week: set aside potable water (start with two gallons per person per day for 14 days) in a closet for your family. For a family of four, that equates to 112 gallons, which is either a space-consuming set of 23 5-gallon jugs or (my recommendation) two 55-gallon rain barrels you can place underneath downspouts on your patio or balcony. Then smile, relax, and tell yourself you are a great person because you've got two weeks of water stored for your family in case of massive tornados, fires, floods, or earthquakes or excessive houseguests.

There are four resources I'd recommend for a sane, calm approach to starting down this path of resilience. First, review the guides I've included in the appendix. Second, consider Chris Martenson's *Crash Course* (peakprosperity.com). While this step-by-step program is designed for individuals and families, it could be scaled up to the neighborhood level with some thought and extra effort. I've read much of Martenson's other material in depth; the team he is assembling is top notch. Third, consider Tess Pennington's excellent Ready Nutrition online community (readynutrition.com).

As National Public Radio has reported, particularly in the *All Things Considered* program, the key to disaster survival is friends and neighbors. The strength of those relationships is what will get us through hard times, and the time to create those new friendships is now.

Which brings us back full circle to the fourth resource for your consideration: your neighbors. If you have not already taken your street through the Map Your Neighborhood program, start there as you begin your personal preparations. You can encourage friends on nearby streets to go through the same mapping process and swap information about skills and equipment, connecting your larger neighborhood together block by block.

After you complete these initial steps, consider creating space in your life to follow your passions via service with local sustainability groups that are building resilience in your bioregion, whether it be supporting your local farmer's market, starting a watershed conversation group, or maintaining bicycle pathways in your neighborhood. As a collection of citizens, if we each follow our passions, the group will naturally get all the basics covered: food, water, shelter, energy, and more.

There are several larger frameworks, or approaches, I'd like you to consider after you have gotten your personal and neighborhood preparations underway. First, politically-oriented readers in small towns and larger subsections of urban areas may be attracted to positively infecting the right people at City Hall with a vision to bring in methodologies for municipalities like *The Natural Step* program by Sarah James (no relation) and Torbjorn Lahti. The program is based on their excellent book *The Natural Step for Communities: How Cities and Towns Can Change to*

Sustainable Practices. The (mostly) unaddressed key to success with approaches like this is both strong neighborhoods and citizen involvement supporting city officials.

Too often a top-down structure of a mayor or city council alone is assumed to be enough impetus for success. After years of public and private efforts, our town only began making significant, critical progress once we allocated a full-time headcount at City Hall under the person of Amber Richards, a positive force of nature who joined the staff after her military career.

This reemergence of local place—the importance of a specific local neighborhood or section of town—is a topic often referred to by architect and social critique James Howard Kunstler: "Contrary to the wishful thinking of Tom Friedman, globalism is winding down. The great contraction leads back to a regional and local reorganization of activity in all nations. The world becomes a bigger place again with more space between the players and a larger array of players as big nations break up into autonomous states. This is really a new phase of history."

A second approach I appreciate has been proposed by Pat Murphy is his enjoyable book *Plan C: Community Survival Strategies.* What I like best about *Plan C* is the focus on practical action that individual citizens and small groups of neighbors can take. Murphy argues that Plan A is continuing down our current unsustainable path toward burning the human race off the face of the planet, with Plan B listed as a massive planet-wide switch to renewable energy sources. Neither feels like something we can significantly affect with our personal lives. But *Plan C*'s focus on changing behaviors, starting with our own and those around us, is not only doable but also leads to a better community to live in here and now.

The third citizen-led framework I am particularly fond of is the Transition Town movement, created by Rob Hopkins (be sure to check out the US-based voice in the Transition conversation, aptly named Transition Voice, curated online by Lindsay and Erik Curren). Although the focus of Transition Town is getting towns away from their oil dependency, the practical implications of Hopkins' ideas inspire a passion for change in many other areas of life. From switching to local food sources to revamping the education of future generations, Transition Towns offer excellent systems with a positive message that counteracts fear and anxiety.

We'll end each chapter with a few ideas to get you motivated and biased towards action. Some tasks will be just for you, others for those you live with, and a few others for to work on with your neighbors. Remember to enjoy yourself!

Actions: Resilience is a worthwhile pursuit; let's start with the all-important steps of the Map Your Neighborhood program:

☐ Gather safety items: bicycle helmet or hardhat, sturdy shoes, leather gloves. Keep them someplace you can easily access at any time – like next to or under your bed.

☐ Get a shut-off wrench for natural gas or propane if you have either at your home. Keep it near the shut off valve.

☐ Know where your water shut off is, and if you need a tool, purchase one to keep near the valve.

☐ If you don't have access to the MYN flipcharts from your local fire department, make Help and OK signs to keep near the front door.

☐ Check your existing fire extinguishers' charge, or purchase the appropriate number for your home. Make sure they're charged and placed appropriately.

☐ Begin a MYN program on your street or if you've already done so, help the next street over get theirs started. Make it a party!

COMMUNITY GARDENS

BALCONY PEA PATCHES

PRESERVING FOOD TOGETHER

FOOD

"Permaculture is revolution disguised as gardening."

Mike Feingold, Educator

From backyard chickens to front porches filled with extra zucchini, food is a great place to begin building resilience into your life. Conversations with neighbors happen naturally over shared meals and swapping of extra foodstuffs.

Lyla came home from another week at the firm where she served as Finance Director. She was weary but excited for the weekend. Her neighbors had invited her and her husband over to celebrate the fall harvest season by creating a meal together made entirely of ingredients from their shared backyard gardens.

She enjoyed the spirited conversations with her neighbors: Nani, a straight-shooting doctor with an artistic flair, and Bill, a former emergency room nurse and current entrepreneur. The four of them had been gardening together and bartering foodstuffs for almost a year and were enjoying this new type of neighborly relationship. They certainly had much to celebrate for the bounty their gardens had produced, and the friendships that had developed.

Lyla also enjoyed seeing how "the other side" did their gardening, as it was a radical departure from her orderly sets of raised beds and precise grid of drip irrigation tubing. Nani and Bill were permaculturalists who seemed to be OK with layers upon layers of different plants growing in close proximity to each other. Nani would always laugh when Lyla made a comment about it, adding her favorite quip, "Variety is a good thing."

Although they'd been neighbors for years, the deeper friendship and gardening partnership began when Nani invited Lyla and the other neighbors on their street over for a winter holiday party to discuss taking care of each other after an earthquake.

Food Builds Bonds

When you and your neighbors agree to check on each other after a natural disaster, you set the stage for positively focused, cooperative projects to succeed—projects like pea patches and modern victory gardens. Nothing builds relationships better than sharing a meal together.

Most major religions involve ritual sharing of meals. The importance of food to our well-being goes beyond the simple nutrition it provides. The state of having food brings us a sense of security. The act of sharing food with others bonds us to them, and growing our own food empowers us.

There's an African saying that the best place to store food is in your neighbor's stomach. This is true no matter what continent you live on. Growing food together and sharing meals as a neighborhood means that when you have to face that emergency, you'll already have built up the relationships that will help you survive the first days, and then rebuild in weeks and months that follow.

A multitude of food-related projects naturally occur after neighbors begin the 'Map Your Neighborhood' conversations. A range of activities, from bartering foodstuffs grown in backyards and balconies to seed swapping with folks at the local feed supply store, cements the emotional bonds that have now begun among neighbors.

Starting Small

Starting out you might be feeling a bit overwhelmed with the ever-growing list of potential projects and preparations to make, both individually and with neighbors. That would be a VERY normal response and leads to an important permaculture principle: To "start small" or take just one baby step at a time.

Permaculture encourages us to start small so we can fail small (we'll get to a fuller definition of permaculture later, but for now think of it as creating systems that mimic nature). Once we learn from our small successes and failures on individual streets in our neighborhoods, we can begin to scale up to the level required to maintain our entire community. We can bring that wisdom to the rest of the neighborhood projects that will naturally roll out of your community conversations. What projects could you start with neighbors to produce small, almost instantaneous results to test and improve before making a larger commitment?

This start-small philosophy is particularly crucial for urban gardeners growing food in the heart of our cities. There is no more inspiring book for this than Novella Carpenter's *Farm City*. From the harsh urban core of Oakland, California, Carpenter entertains and educates the reader on food production and raising animals on a city block scale. When thinking about ideal food-related animals in an urban environment, consider the relatively quiet hen (just say No to roosters), rabbits (which can reach a harvest age as fast as chickens), and quail (which have very tasty little eggs). Most municipalities now have easy-to-find code documenting how many and what type of animals you are allowed to keep within city limits.

While the direct health benefits of producing your own food are significant, the societal benefits of a neighborhood producing its own food are even more considerable. Permaculture's three primary goals match up perfectly with the focus of Prepared Neighborhoods:

1. Take care of the planet (let's start with our street).

2. Take care of people (let's start with our neighbors).

3. Share the surplus (a great way to build community!).

Growing Up

Smaller urban environments encourage our creativity when looking for additional growing space. There are many folks experimenting with growing food in a vertical fashion right now, from retrofitting apartment balconies to new construction of high-rises. Particularly in Europe, we're seeing a number of metropolitan reforestation projects undertaken with the construction of new skyscrapers (two ideas that normally do not mesh well together). An example project in Italy has been nicknamed a "Vertical Forest" and was completed in 2014. Look up the photos online for inspiration; architect Stefano Boeri's design fit

900+ trees and 2000+ plants into two residential towers. That's quite a bit of food.

In New York, the Brooklyn Grange rooftop farms have made quite a name for themselves, showing just how exciting food production projects in urban environments can be with the world's largest green rooftop farm. Spanning two acres of rooftops, they grow 50,000+ pounds of organic produce each year. That's not a typo. 50,000 pounds annually and they are expanding. Granted, there are 2.5+ million people living in Brooklyn who need to be fed, but the ability to produce this much food on previously unused roof space is tremendous.

On a smaller scale but still appropriate to city dwellers are columnar fruit trees, sometimes referred to as "urban fruit trees." These hybrid species require only a very small area—literally no more of a footprint than a large pot—due to a focus on vertical rather than broad growth. With easy training, they develop tall crowns instead of spreading branches, which bring an elegance and visual appeal to them that is unique. Do a quick Google image search on them; they are quite beautiful. Columnar trees are a good example of the fastest growing segment in permaculture, an urban focus that does a judo move on the idea of "limiting constraints" within a city, using those constraints to fuel imaginative solutions.

Consider how many of your neighbors a two-acre plot could feed during and after a wide-scale emergency. Think about the myriad of other benefits rooftop farming could provide your city: better use of tight spaces, lowering summer temperatures, cleaning water without chemical treatment plants, diverting food scraps from landfills, and, of course, healthier, fresher food for the neighborhood.

While suburban and exurban residents can certainly take advantage of several vertical growing techniques as well, we can look to Weston, Massachusetts as a classic small-town example of what to do when you and your neighbors have access to more space. Author, professor, environmentalist, and community farmer Brian Donohue recorded his town's journey in his how-to book on "suburban sustainability" titled *Reclaiming the Commons.*

In the book's foreword, fellow author and environmentalist Wes Jackson connects the reader's individual desire to lessen human impact on the environment with the suburban neighborhood in which the reader resides. Food production gardens may be started in individual backyards and condominium rooftops, but when the scale is increased just slightly, to the point of the neighborhood, wonderful things begin to happen. The people of Weston have been doing this for decades.

Donohue makes two significant proposals in his book. First, suburban towns must prioritize the acquisition and protection of native land (that could be forest, prairie, or mountain depending on the bioregion) as well as farmland. Second, that protected land should then be *actively and sustainably engaged.* This points to an excellent "bridge approach" to land spanning the zones of rural, exurban, and suburban.

Similar lessons can be drawn from Donohue's book for

applicability to our urban environments. Just as Seattle did with the Beacon Hill project, all cities would do well to prioritize the acquisition and sustainable engagement with open spaces. Staying true to the permaculture principle of starting small, think about what open area of your own space you could experiment with for growing food. You may only have a single wall of a home or apartment building, but if that wall gets decent sun exposure, you could experiment with growing food vertically on trellises and harvesting rainwater from the roof for irrigation.

Choosing Crops

Once you've decided to begin, even with just a small space, which crops should you start with? Steve Solomon, the founder of Territorial Seed Company, has an excellent book called 'Gardening When It Counts' that ranks vegetables by how difficult they are to grow and includes a thorough explanation of the importance of root systems as a key to successful gardening. Solomon assumes the reader has never before gardened and walks us through the basics, from the selection of seeds and seedlings to proper care of hand tools.

(Confession: I immediately went out and re-sharpened my gardening tools after reading his "Tools and Tasks" chapter!)

The Resilient Gardener by Carol Deppe is also well worth your reading time, whether you are an experienced food gardener or not. It goes into significant detail on what she considers to be the five essential basics: potatoes, corn, beans, squash, and eggs. But Deppe also goes well beyond the basics that more experienced gardeners will appreciate, like how to select crops based on dealing with the weirdness of weather patterns due to climate change in your area and the cost/benefit ratio of different types of gardening in terms of labor versus output (I'm looking at you, double-dug garden beds!).

One key aspect to choosing which crops to cultivate is to ask your local garden and feed supply store what works best in your climate. The folks who work there will quickly become your new best friends with their deep experience in your specific area.

Protein Posse

The island where I live (classified primarily as "exurban," occupying the space between suburban and rural classifications) has seen success beyond the cultivation of fruits and vegetables with the addition of small flocks of animals rotated on borrowed, empty lots and fields. Running under the nickname the "Protein Posse," this ad hoc group of both professional and hobbyist micro-ranchers are leveraging small pieces of land that previously sat unused. Placing animals such as sheep, goats, and chickens on these parcels enhance both the land's beauty and fertility, as well as producing delicious eggs, meats, and more. Novella Carpenter's book details examples of Oakland's own version of a Protein Posse in an urban environment.

Russ Berg of our island's Protein Posse explains, "Meat that comes from local animals simply tastes better. You really can tell a difference when the animal has been raised and cared for by people who truly appreciate all the great things that animal brings to the world. Whether it's wool, meat, milk, eggs, or even their manure to help grow vegetables, animal husbandry is an important part of a local strong town."

Backyard egg production has skyrocketed in the past decade, matched only by the resurgence of modern-day victory gardens. Many books at the library can provide step-by-step instructions for siting and building a proper chicken coop, whether for two birds or twenty. Although you should be prepared to fight local ordinances limiting the number of birds you can keep depending on your zoning, you'll find that sharing fresh eggs will make you fast friends in your neighborhood. Just avoid keeping a rooster in your flock.

Jo Ann Trick, the brains behind Bainbridge Island's self-guided chicken coop tour, explained: "Raising chickens is a fun and economical answer to producing food. With little human input, chickens will supply families with food, compost for the garden, and daily entertainment." For years, Jo Ann has taken this backyard entertainment and infused it with a strong sense of community with her *"Tour de Coop"* annual fundraiser by connecting neighbors who are building resilience into their lives. After just a few stops on the Tour, the encouraging conversations and interesting coop architecture give neighbors a strong feeling that they too can raise chickens.

If you have access to grass, whether it's a large pasture or a shared lawn with your duplex neighbor, any of the books by Joel Salatin or Andy Lee will inspire and instruct you on the construction of movable chicken "tractors" to keep your birds healthy, happy, and secure. In my mind, this is the only justification for keeping a lawn!

Celebration

In a similar vein as Berry, you'll also find Barbara Kingsolver's popular *Animal, Vegetable, Miracle* inspiring, educational and full of practical (and poignant) anecdotes. She and her family are committed to only purchasing food grown in their own neighborhood—or their own backyard—for an entire year. One theme running through her book that is crucial for citizens creating their own Prepared Neighborhood is that of celebration. At one point, Kingsolver assembled an amazing birthday celebration by recruiting food inputs from her local neighbors and farmers.

Imagine the excitement among your neighbors about creating food security if they experienced the following description of Kingsolver's gathering:

"We set up a sound system on the back patio, dragged bales of straw into benches, and eyed the sky, which threatened rain all day Saturday but by late afternoon had not delivered. We carried a horse trough out of the barn and filled it with ice to chill our Virginia Chambourcin and Misty River wines, and beer from a nearby microbrewery. The lamb kabobs on the grill made all our mouths water for an hour while Kay and her helpers worked their mojo in our kitchen. The food, when it came out, was applauded: the summer rolls were saucy, the lamb succulent, the frittata puffy and light. The strawberry-rhubarb crisp vanished into thin air. Here's what we *didn't* have: the shrimp arranged in a ring. like pink poker chips; those rock-hard broccoli wedges and lathed carrots surrounding the ubiquitous white dip; the pile of pineapple and melon chunks on a platter. Nobody seemed too disappointed."

Building Community

The benefits aren't just for our communities. A more intimate relationship with our food directly benefits us as individuals as well. Laura Lyon of ModernVictoryGarden.com says, "I personally relish having an excuse to slow my life down from the frantic pace of modern life. I think many of us that are Type A personalities feel vaguely uncomfortable with the idea of just 'doing nothing'. While I value and appreciate rest and relaxation, the truth is I actually 'relax' more if I also feel like there is still something 'productive' happening. It's kind of sad really that I feel that way, but it is the truth."

She continues, "Gardening and cooking meals using the bounty of the garden results in a valuable contribution to my family's well-being. The fact that I can provide that value while moving at a much slower pace, enjoying being outdoors, dressed in comfortable clothes, and taking lots of breaks to just admire and wonder at the science and magic that a garden represents is pretty amazing stuff."

As we scale success in individual victory gardens and pea patches up to the neighborhood level, we are able to access an exciting new set of projects that build community (while producing delicious foodstuffs). Imagine a homeowners' association that aspires to more than a repetitive sea of unproductive landscaping. What would happen if they brought in their own professional farmer to work the last two remaining vacant lots and mentor neighbors on their own shared vegetable gardens? What would happen if the neighborhood's "green thumb," who converted her front lawn into a beautiful food forest, was asked to do the same for several of her neighbors' lawns? Imagine the joy of creating and buying your own produce within walking distance of your home?

That's just what happened in 2014 when Sarah Sailer extended her significant gardening talents from her own 1/5 acre yard in downtown Loveland, Colorado to also include more than half a dozen of her neighbors' yards. They formed their own unique take on a CSA (Community Supported Agriculture) called Plenty Farms, with the most excellent tagline of "reviving the local village; sharing the wealth of food." This is a "farm" unlike any other, as it's divided amongst the six front yards and goes beyond the traditional CSA mixture of vegetables and fruits to include sourdough bread, herbs, and flowers, all grown within their urban neighborhood.

As we begin our path to preparedness with our individual homes—whether they are single family houses or denser apartment complexes—we've learned that, just as in the planting of the Three Sisters, the community created by neighbors joining together via Prepared Neighborhoods will bring a sense of true resilience. As we repeat the Three Sisters process, connecting streets to each other and neighborhoods to other neighborhoods, we'll find the entire town entering a state of calm preparedness while enjoying a new sense of community.

Emergency Food Storage

Think through what happens in an extended emergency: food deliveries are cut off. Grocery stores are empty in three days (or less). People's pantries and refrigerators are empty two days later (after the electricity goes out, refrigerated food will only last six hours and frozen food about 48 hours). Your neighbors will begin to stop by to see if they can borrow food, and of course, you are going to share what you have. Depending on the number of neighbors you have, your food stores will rapidly dwindle from one year's worth to one week's worth.

The only positive solution is to encourage those neighbors also to build up their food stores, as well as be prepared to share with others.

Laying in extra food, water, and medical supplies for your neighbors keeps your mindset positive and solution-focused. By helping your neighbors, you are also helping the first responders in your area who are working to repair the core infrastructure of your town. You are now part of the solution, rather than being the problem.

The brief rule of thumb for emergency food storage is to start with two weeks, eventually building up to 12 months. If you have the resources to do bulk purchasing, your shopping can be completed in a single concentrated weekend. For those of us who need more time to build up emergency food stores, it is useful to reallocate your weekly budget to buy two of everything you would normally buy one of in terms of durable goods like dry, canned, and preserved goods. Set the extras aside, and when you've collected enough to fill a five-gallon bucket, take a few minutes to seal it properly.

Proper storage of food for long-term preservation is not difficult and does not need to be expensive. Storage options include sealed Mylar bags placed inside food-grade five-gallon buckets with oxygen remover packets thrown in. Many of these materials can be purchased in bulk with your direct neighbors or others in your town.

If you can, buy and store what you normally eat, rather than prepared rations that you've never tried before. During the high emotional stress of a natural or human-made disaster, we don't want to introduce additional physical distress to our bodies; it is the time for comfort food.

Several excellent books examine how individuals and families can store away emergency foodstuffs to build resilience into their lives for short-term emergencies, particularly Peggy Layton's *Emergency Food Storage & Survival Handbook* and Daisy Luther's *The Pantry Primer: A Prepper's Guide to Whole Food on a Half-Price Budget.*

While it is preferable to buy what you normally eat, it might not be the most practical, and the important thing is that you have sufficient calories and nutrition to get you through the crisis. Freeze-dried camping-style rations are designed to provide nutritionally complete foods that are easy to store and that last. You can purchase amounts from single meals to two-week pre-packed buckets.

The Emergency Essentials Premier bucket feeds one person for two weeks at 1,900 calories per day. Three buckets feed two people for two weeks at 2,700 per day. My camping buddies say that Mountain House foods are the best tasting. ThePrepared.com has an excellent in-depth review of the "Best Two-Week Emergency Survival Foods." Share this list with your neighbors, and build a community store with a variety of foods and supplements for everyone. And don't forget vegetarians and anyone with food allergies or intolerances, like being gluten-free.

Cultivate Your Own Garden

For do-it-yourselfers, small-scale fruit and vegetable gardening can turn a rewarding hobby into a more resilient way of life. Citizens typically choose one of two paths when first experimenting with growing their own food. The first method is via raised beds, popularized by the effusive Mel Bartholomew and others in his now-classic Square-Foot Gardening technique. His book of the same title (get the more recent "all-new" version updated in 2005; the original is from 1981) takes you step by step through the creation of new garden beds, planting, and harvesting.

After much trial and error, Bartholomew found 4' x 4' garden beds to be ideal, with the average arm reach of a person – young or old – to be about 2'. By eliminating wasteful practices backyard gardeners were following as they sought to do simply scaled down versions of professional farming, Bartholomew found he could also grow the same amount of food in just 20 percent of the space. For urban and suburban gardeners, that 80 percent reduction in space requirements means you can tuck a fully functioning vegetable garden in many more spaces. This technique also encourages gardeners to stagger their plantings so they can stagger their harvests, seeking balance in both.

Years ago I became acquaintances with one such person (I think of her as the ultimate raised bed gardener), the purveyor of the recently retired ModernVictoryGarden.com, Laura Lyon. Laura is a "numbers person" at work, detailed and meticulous, and with one glance at her substantial gardens, you can see how she translates those skills into her gardening (it also translates well to her blog–the archives are well worth a visit). With an ultra-efficient use of space and materials, Laura produces a tremendous amount of food for her family each year on a relatively small amount of land.

One day when we were trading tree collards, an odd but

delicious version of kale that passes from gardener to gardener via cuttings rather than seed (it does not grow "true" from seed and rarely even goes to seed), I asked Laura about her approach to gardening.

She told me, "My garden is not just a hobby. I definitely enjoy it and find great pleasure in the time I spend in the garden, but I have a definite purpose to what I do. My primary objective is to feed this household with all of our vegetable needs and as much of our fruit as is possible, and to do it in a fashion that is economical, significantly less reliant on fossil fuels, and produces food that is nutrient dense and of a quality surpassing that which I could acquire even from local suppliers. The challenge is to do this in my 'spare' time and within the limiting factors of my property and location."

Preserving Your Harvest

For those times when your garden does produce an overabundance–and it will happen often–follow Bartholomew's book up with a read through of Janet Chadwick's excellent (and inexpensive) reference book, *The Busy Person's Guide to Preserving Food*. You'll be surprised at just how much food a small portion of land can produce during your growing months to then enjoy throughout the year. Believe me, a sweet dried fig in the middle of the winter goes a long way to raising your spirits as you wait for the return of the sun (can you tell I live near Seattle?). If gardening is just not your thing, you can still benefit from a neighbor's green thumb by offering to help them with preservation.

Our food preservation methods of choice are dehydration, freezing, and when the bounty forces it upon us, canning. We've made the time/monetary investments in both solar and electric dehydrators as well as a large chest freezer, which pay for themselves within the first year when you consider the prices of organic fruits and meats from the grocery store. Using a heated canning process is a longstanding tradition with food preservation. Given the amount of work and mess it generates, this is best done with neighbors, to share the workload. You'll have plenty of time to deepen the relationships with those hours of conversation!

Fermentation is a particularly fun method of preservation, from sauerkraut to kombucha. My wife makes batches of amazing fermented ginger carrots that taste out of this world. An hour's worth of her preservation time makes enough fermented carrots to keep us healthy for months. We both enjoy making our own kefir and kombucha to share with friends, with a gentle—but oh so serious—spousal rivalry going between sugar-based kombucha and honey-based kombucha (referred to as Jun). Other preservation methods you can explore include smoking, salting, and cold storage.

Cold storage is the use of root (e.g. potatoes, carrots) cellars and fruit cellars on traditional farms and rural homesteads. Gardeners in urban and suburban environments can also pursue this low/no electricity method of food preservation. If you do have the space for a shared cellar, this makes for a fantastic neighborhood project. If space does not allow, grab an inexpensive humidity and temperature gauge at your local hardware store and wander around your building taking measurements. I've found near-ideal conditions in locations near HVAC equipment (especially near heat pump equipment that blows a consistent flow of cool air), and cold northeastern corners of basements and low storage areas.

Look for spots with a consistently cool temperature (55°F) and high humidity (90 percent). Storing foodstuffs in rodent-proof containers in these areas accomplishes the same goal as a root or fruit cellar. For storage of dry items such as beans and grains, seek out the same cool temperatures but without the high humidity.

Back to your own space: even if you have limited space you still have several options for producing food during good and bad times. If you have a south-facing wall, create a second "wall" in front of it with a soil-filled wood pallet (use weed cloth to keep the soil in place) to hold plants or a series of smaller terracotta pots and larger wooden wine barrels in front of that heat absorbing wall. Your plants will be happy to produce more than normal amounts with that sun orientation.

You can extend the growing surface of the wine barrels by cutting numerous holes on the sides of them (they'll maintain their structural integrity), inserting a good-sized seedling into each hole. Add a center column made of a perforated tube or durable mesh bag and you now have a repository for food scraps from your kitchen that will turn into compost. Consider buying a small amount of composting worms from your local nursery to kick-start the composting process; they'll happily move back and forth between the compost area and the soil supporting the plants. Add collecting dishes beneath all the pots and barrels to reuse the nutrient-laden water that trickles through.

Composting kitchen scraps divert a significant source of potential greenhouse gas from landfills and give you a free renewable source of nutrient-rich compost to improve your soil. While rural, exurban, and suburban have enough space to implement traditional compost bins – particularly when sharing maintenance duties with neighbors – urban citizens often find themselves with plenty of kitchen scraps but no place to put them. Thankfully, there are a number of vermicomposting systems (vermi = worms) that are designed specifically for apartment dwellers. One clever example is the Biovessel: an indoor ecosystem that accepts your daily food scraps, allowing worms to transform it into compost, and is beautiful enough to keep on your kitchen counter.

Community Gardening

This new relationship we can have with our food does not need to be reserved only for times of emergency. Other than rotating out and replacing stored foodstuffs at the appropriate times, the majority of food-related projects a prepared neighborhood can undertake will involve getting your hands dirty, which is half the fun!

Lean economic times expose the flaws in wasting resources to plant, water, and maintain an ornamental "cherry" tree. Although the real cherry or plum tree can be messy, there is a beauty about them that an ornamental "plum" tree will never have. In this new economic reality, we need every available plant that can produce food to do so, whether in the middle of an urban core area or out in the countryside or the balcony of your apartment. We can remove and compost the ornamental fruit trees and replace them with those that actually produce a crop. Kids can learn that cherries come from those messy pink-hued trees rather than the grocery store and that they have to race against the birds to get the ripe ones in time!

Locally produced food is significantly healthier than crops harvested well before their prime in order to make the long journey to the store without bruising. Decentralized food production has radical advantages over centralized in terms of carbon output, job creation, and quality of life for all involved. Increasingly, resources like Sound Food – a Washington state organization that promotes local food – are popping up in municipalities across North America, with updated locations for local food sources, from professional farms to backyard operations.

In addition, we can start this food revolution in our own neighborhoods! I asked Carolyn Goodwin, founder of Sound Food, to tell me more. She explained that establishing relationships with the farmers in your town and the surrounding communities is another great way to prepare for a food emergency.

Many area farmers are now harvesting year-round thanks to hoop houses and other season extenders, so even during an emergency, as long as they can still grow and harvest food, farmers are more likely to honor commitments to their existing customers. Joining a CSA (Community Supported Agriculture) program is a good way to ensure you have access to fresh produce, eggs, and even meat during an extended emergency or directly after a short-term one. Carolyn added: "Farmers can also help stock your emergency food storage. Several farmers local to me have special winter-storage offerings in the fall. Every year, I sign up for a bulk order of potatoes, onions, and garlic. It lasts well into the spring in an unheated downstairs storage room."

As Carolyn referenced, preserving the harvest is another way to add to your stock inexpensively and with the highest quality of food. Canned, dried and fermented foods can be stored for long periods of time without refrigeration. Many local garden or feed stores in urban, suburban, and rural areas offer classes to learn how to preserve safely.

As part of your Map Your Neighborhood efforts, you can also find out who in your neighborhood might have preservation equipment such as canners and dehydrators. Try hosting a canning party–it's a great way to divide the labor and get to know your neighbors.

Neighbors can start small and work together, encouraging one another to grow a variety of lettuces and other small vegetables in containers on porches and balconies, and then expand from there. Those in larger dwelling complexes can rent space (very inexpensively) at local "pea patches" to begin growing larger items. There are many cases around the country where neighbors on a street with a vacant lot transformed it into an urban vegetable garden (with or without permission of the absentee owner!). I found Novella Carpenter's *Farm City* book particularly inspiring on this topic.

Her delightful writing is full of conversation snippets with a wide variety of characters she encounters on her journey to a farm in the middle of a dense urban environment. One such conversation discussed the use of open space as vegetable gardens in the middle of the nineteenth century Paris. A concentration of small lots in an area of the city called Le Marais produced 100,000+ tons of food each year... so much that the Parisians were able to export the extra foodstuffs to nearby countries.

While that project was completed with the cooperation of Paris officials, Novella's autobiographical tale of creating a farm in the middle of Oakland, California was done without any official endorsement from municipal officials (she did get the grudging approval of her landlord).

But not everyone needs to be as courageous as Novella. Neighbors with enough space and local leadership can recruit a professional farmer or a permaculture consultant to set up a shared vegetable garden for their street or complex. Groups can organize composting systems to eliminate significant waste streams by transforming grass clippings and yard debris into valuable garden inputs, all within walking distance of their homes. Citizens can combine efforts of several streets for a larger scale neighborhood-wide project, like planting an orchard of nut and fruit trees.

Planting an orchard may seem like a monumental,

expensive task, but by dividing the cost among a 200-person condominium complex or five streets of 20 homes, the investment cost per person plummets, as well as the workload. Even if you aren't doing the gardening yourself, you can still enjoy the fruits (literally) of others doing so. Recent "cottage kitchen" legislation in some states is now allowing foodstuffs to be produced legally at the home and neighborhood level. And, of course, there are still many "illegal" neighborhood stands where barter and local transactions for locally produced food items are thriving. Just don't let the code enforcement officer catch you!

Anita Rockefeller, a retired EPA Director and pea patch proprietor on Bainbridge Island, WA, shared with me the backstory of the community pea patch she and her husband Phil (the Washington State Senator) began for their neighborhood. In the fall of 2008, they anticipated local food banks' need for more food than in past years due to the economic recession and rising unemployment.

The garden they created is all organic—no synthetic pesticides or fertilizers are used—resulting in healthy fruit trees, vegetables, and some lovely flowers to support pollinating bees. The local parks department discovered the community garden and now includes it on their walking tours.

When I asked Anita about her vision for the space, she explained, "We had a large space with good sun on our property that wasn't being used productively and we decided a community garden would be a practical way to raise food for the local food bank."

We discussed her goals for the project as they have

morphed over the years. Anita told me, "The number one goal of the garden from the time it opened in 2009 is that participants would grow for themselves as well as to help others. The second and third goals were to help people learn how food is grown (gaining a greater appreciation for farmers), and to connect neighbors with one another ... learning from each other and creating a sense of community."

Permaculture

An approach to growing food well suited to small neighborhoods, permaculture is an approach to food production that mimics natural ecosystems through symbiotic groupings among plants. To be clear, you can take most of the learning from Square Foot Gardening and apply it to permaculture beds as well.

Chuck Estin of Bios Design, a permaculture designer who now lives in Hawaii, designed my backyard "food forest" (an edible garden that mimics the natural layers in a forest). He explains how permaculture works: "By observing patterns in nature, we can apply those same patterns to our own existence as humans living in a community. For instance, we see in nature patterns of centralization and decentralization."

He also explains the relationship between decentralization and centralization that is key to a permaculture system: "Growing food in a decentralized manner allows for a greater abundance that is more secure than growing all the food for our island on one central farm that may be struck by tragedy. Yet we also see the benefits of centralization when thinking about a marketing cooperative of local farmers that enhances their sales and increases the volume of local food for the community."

Look in the gardening section of your local bookstore for titles on growing your own food in a beautiful and productive manner and you'll find important books on permaculture by David Holmgren and others. But the best two to start with are Toby Hemenway's *Gaia's Garden: A Guide to Home-Scale Permaculture* and the newer *Practical Permaculture: for Home Landscapes, Your Community, and the Whole Earth* by Jessi Bloom and Dave Boehnlein.

With chapters that range from gardening in a city to creating communities for the garden, the techniques in these books are appropriate for any piece of land, from larger pieces in rural and exurban zoning to smaller suburban lots and clever uses of roofs, patios and shared urban spaces.

When he is not writing, Boehnlein can usually be found teaching. He is the Education Director at the infamous Bullocks Brothers Permaculture Homestead on Orcas Island, an idyllic island community in the Pacific Northwest, and also happens to be my own permaculture teacher.

But this approach to gardening is not relegated to rural islands; permaculture thrives in urban environments as well. Witness the Beacon Food Forest that sits on seven acres in the middle of Seattle, one of the largest permaculture installations in a major city. My friend Jenny Pell—a brilliant designer who moved in recent years from Seattle to Maui—was part of the design team for this significant undertaking.

The location serves as a hub for education with cleverly named fun classes such as *"The Joy of Chickens"* and *"A Meal for Two: You and Your Microbiomes,"* as well as a source of food for community regulars (classic pea patches are available) and visitors (plenty of snackable items as you tour the location, which changes depending on the season). In fact, foraging is encouraged.

(If foraging is your thing, be sure to check out the *Falling Fruit* website, a citizen-driven online database of forage-friendly sites of fruit and nut trees near you.)

As most urban environments include a diversity of ethnicity, when raising money for the project, the volunteers mailed over 6,000 postcards in five languages to the area neighborhoods. The Co-founder of the Beacon Food Forest, Glenn Herlihy, commented: "There are Vietnamese, Chinese, Filipinos, and Africans in the area. It is a place where all ages and ethnicities can meet; a food system being developed in a neighborhood that's looking for more self-reliance. It's getting people together by having a common denominator: soil."

In fact, you could argue that food production schemes in urban neighborhoods have a major advantage over more rural neighborhoods: a potentially enormous set of volunteers. The community at Beacon Hill shares both gardening chores and gardening decisions. With a steering committee of about a dozen citizens who often host listening groups to solicit consensus, they create their own rules and regulations for work parties to then enact. When you see a work party of 100+ people show up on an early Saturday morning in the cold Seattle drizzle, you know you're finding widespread neighborhood support!

Hemenway's book even has a specific chapter on permaculture gardening in the city, addressing the specific challenges an urban environment presents to a group of neighbors seeking to create food security. Multi-functionality is his recommended approach to spaces that must serve the needs of various groups for traffic, recreation, and food production.

For example, Hemenway describes the dismay he first felt at the lack of space for his many favorite fruit trees when he moved from a 10-acre rural lot to a 50' x 100' urban lot. Much to his surprise, as he reached out to his new neighbors, he discovered each had a few fruit trees of their own that produced an abundance of fruit to share. By selecting species that his neighbors did not already have, Hemenway added to the overall food production level and diversity of the neighborhood and made lifelong friends in the process.

In addition to neighbors working "better together" on shared projects, as you get deeper into permaculture, you'll learn about other "better together" combination techniques such as the Three Sisters, in which corn, beans, and squash are planted together. The corn shoots up first, providing a structure for the beans to climb—a structure that the gardener did not need to build. In the meantime, the squash is covering the surrounding ground with its huge leaves to provide effective weed control, which the gardener did not have to perform. When planted together, all three plants end up stronger and more bountiful, with less labor required of the gardener.

Anita Rockefeller offered a replacement for the squash in the Three Sisters combination, "Particularly in the wet Pacific Northwest, the squash needs little water while the corn and beans require quite a bit. If you are watering the others as needed, the squash will get powdery mildew and rot. Instead, consider a leafy lettuce, chard, or beets in place of squash."

You can begin your own permaculture experiments like these this weekend by yourself or with a "green thumb" neighbor. As you seek to deepen your knowledge beyond books and blogs, consider taking a Permaculture Design Certificate (PDC) course. These can be completed either in person or online. The in-person PDCs usually require a two to four weeks on-site "edu-vacation," which are loads of fun (and hard work). If taking a break from work and life duties for a few weeks is not possible, consider an online PDC. Google "Geoff Lawton" and you'll find a good-looking Australian fellow wearing his ubiquitous bush hat with a ready smile. His online courses are wildly popular and you'll be able to find fellow students in your bioregion to connect with through the course's forums.

Swapping & Sharing

Neighbors within walking distance of each other can harvest and exchange produce at the peak of ripeness, with no need to worry about fruits or vegetables being bruised or destroyed during transit. We've had years of direct experience with our micro-farm partners, walking through open space forest to swap produce, whey, and tools among our exurban homes. It brings joy, creates community, and—compared to grocery store produce—provides significantly healthier food at a fraction of the cost.

One of our micro-farm partners is a mainstay on our island's network of value-add farms, Nancy and Bob Fortner of Sweetlife Farm. Nancy, a no-nonsense former nurse, has a spunky, irresistible personality and a lot to say about the food sharing: "A town lives or dies by its usefulness to its inhabitants and each person's perception of having an important role in it. In an emergency, usefulness is defined by access to food, shelter, and medical attention. Daily usefulness can be as simple as feeling needed, nurtured, and supported by neighbors and nearby friends. It is the straight-up knowing that there is a safety net of people you can count on for a two-way sharing of not just locally produced wholesome food, but also time, teaching, ideas, values, and kindness. 'Food' is something we all give to one another and is necessary, whether it comes from good dirt or good soul."

Our conversation went beyond the sharing of food into a larger discussion of simply sharing. There is a truism that sharing food is the basis of all that is good in relationships. Most religions have communal dining at the core of their activities, right next to worship.

I loved Nancy's insight: "The measurement of a community

is how well it feeds the souls along with the stomachs of its citizens. We are both securely planted in the 'retirement' stage of our lives, yet have chosen a lifestyle that requires constant physical and mental effort. I am humbled knowing that our ability to contribute to the fabric of our community and continue to grow food for ourselves and turn some of it into products we sell depends on both our perceived value in our community as individuals and as a business and, increasingly, the willingness of friends to pitch in and help us complete never-ending tasks."

That last sentiment Nancy refers to is an annual winter holiday sale they host at their farm. Like many other farms around the country, a significant portion of the revenue of their farm flows into their business over this short three-day event. Nancy and Bob (a retired nurse and physician, respectively) make up the sum total of their farm's full-time employees. Just as food swapping lends itself to deeper relationships with neighbors, so does voluntary service to favorite farms. Nancy commented, "We quite literally couldn't pull it off without a lot of help that is freely offered and gratefully accepted. We need this community and we want it to need us."

The sense of community that is built by sharing food—particularly homegrown food—builds resilience into our relationships. For more on the long-term intangible benefits of focusing on local food production, check out Wendell Berry's *Bringing It to the Table* from your local library. I particularly found his discussion of "balance" poignant. When you attempt to grow a portion of your own food, you and your neighbors quickly notice—firsthand, right in front of you—any imbalances in the systems you are creating.

Through small experiments we seek this balance, discovering the optimum ratio of:

1. people to land, and

2. plants to animals.

For instance, too many people working too small of a plot of land leads to boredom and not enough produce to share. But too few people working that same plot of land can lead to an overburdened set of workers who lose enthusiasm for the project.

Berry explores this physical labor aspect even deeper: "Physical exertion for any useful purpose is looked down upon; it is permissible to work hard for 'sport' or 'recreation,' but to make any practical use of the body is considered beneath dignity." This speaks to a common response I've heard from folks not yet growing food themselves, as they tour the garden of other people. "Goodness, what hard work," I hear them often exclaim. And yet those same individuals think nothing of spending 90 minutes at the gym or yoga studio.

Actions: It's time to celebrate with food!

- [ ] Find out if you have any restrictions on which/how many animals you are allowed to keep.

- [ ] Lay in emergency food storage for two weeks for yourself and loved ones, eventually building up to 12 months so you can offer charity to others.

- [ ] Plant smaller fruits and vegetable gardens in any spaces available to you. Consider replacing the lawn and ornamental plants with those that bear food!

- [ ] Preserve overabundance for winter/emergencies.

- [ ] Solicit one or more other neighbors' interest in planting a larger scale, community-focused fruit orchard and/or vegetable garden.

- [ ] Explore options for raising shared animals together as neighbors.

WATER CISTERNS AND BARRELS

HOW-TO WORKSHOPS

FILTERS AND PURIFIERS

WATER

"In many places, the water supply chain from source to tap is long and made of many delicate links. If a cow steps on the supply line, pump breaks, a wire works loose, the electricity goes out, the city misplaces your check, or there is a natural disaster, your water flow could stop."

Art Ludwig
Ecological systems designer and author

The rule of thumb among wilderness experts is that humans can survive for three weeks without food, but only three days without water. A widespread natural disaster will not only interrupt your current water source, it could contaminate it for weeks/months to come. Having multiple methods for securing potable water is crucial for every neighborhood.

Sam was furious. As his "guests" departed, Sam found himself biting his tongue to stop the flow of unkind words running through his mind from becoming audible. He had just been curtly informed by representatives from the local golf course that water rationing for the entire neighborhood was to begin immediately.

The golf course—which shared the same group well system as Sam's neighborhood—was using its clout to grab the lion's share of water allocation so they could keep their fairways green during the late summer heat bearing down on the town. This spelled disaster for the neighborhood's younger fruit trees and vegetable gardens.

Sam knew the amount of water he needed each month to run through his 1/2-acre food garden's drip irrigation system. The rationing limit would mean a significant loss of food for his family and zero surplus to share with the rest of his neighborhood.

After taking a few deep breaths to calm himself, Sam pulled out his smartphone and began researching rain harvesting techniques and water cisterns.

"At least I'll be ready for next year," he said aloud to himself. The pair of milking goats nearby paused to look at him curiously, then returned to munching on their hay.

The Precious Resource

In the last chapter, we discussed the importance of food—both producing it and storing it at individual and neighborhood levels—to build resilience in a community. Every good discussion of gardening and food production needs a reality check on one of the primary requirements to grow food: water. In addition to requiring clean water for food production—especially in the summer months—we also need potable water to maintain our own health during an emergency.

North American towns usually have a mixture of water sources, from personal wells to professionally managed public systems pulling water from a nearby river or reservoir. But an unpolluted source of this basic life element is becoming increasingly scarce in many areas of North America. Whether a neighborhood is facing a short-term emergency like an earthquake or a long-term emergency like the 2012 drought that affected our entire country, the same cooperative planning is useful to ensure a steady flow of potable water.

But sometimes we have the opposite problem of a drought: too much water, due to flooding or storm surge. We'll discuss solutions to both of these problems as we learn about the process of water reclamation (either one-time or ongoing), purification, storage, and finally, redistribution. As we bridge the gap from individual systems for houses and multi-unit dwellings to large connected systems in the heart of a city, we'll find the sweet spot once again is the neighborhood.

Not Enough Water

In recent natural disasters, we've often seen citizens wasting significant amounts of fuel and personal energy driving around looking for bottled water (unsuccessfully, most of the time). A small investment of planning time would have saved them quite a bit of trouble, and enabled them to better use their resources to help their area recover more quickly.

Storage Amounts

We begin with individual planning that every member of a neighborhood can do on their own. The rule of thumb of at least "one gallon per person per day" is antiquated. Consider doubling or tripling that amount for a real emergency where you'll need fresh water for cleaning wounds, staying hydrated during strenuous recovery activities, and cleaning up. Add even more if you have pets or other animals in your life.

It is easy to calculate how many gallons of water to set aside. Store at least two weeks of potable water (more, if possible, to share with others) in an area that has a good chance of surviving an earthquake (e.g. not on a high, unsecured shelf). Use clean containers that are noncorrosive, tightly covered, and easy to lift. A gallon of water weighs over eight pounds, so even a small five-gallon container is going to weigh over 40 pounds when full.

For a family of four, two gallons per person per day for 14 days equates to 112 gallons, which is either a space-consuming set of 23 5-gallon jugs or (perhaps a better use of space) two 55-gallon water or rain barrels. Because a full 55-gallon water barrel weighs 450 pounds, you won't want to move it once it's full. For a rain barrel, place it underneath a downspout on your patio or balcony, and keep a water purification method on hand. For a water barrel you'll fill with a hose, place it somewhere with a solid foundation—which is not necessarily your garage. Using a drinking water hose, rinse the barrel with water only, then add five gallons. Add enough water preserver concentrate for the full 55 gallons. Cover barrel loosely and slosh around to mix. Remove cover and fill to 2-3" from the top. Replace cover and tighten cap using a bung wrench for an airtight seal. Mark the date you filled the barrel and the expiration date (five years). Store hand pump with the barrel.

Keep in mind that even with doubling the "one gallon per person per day" rule, you will need a radical reduction in your normal water usage habits: Americans use an average of 160 gallons of water per person per day. Even with a careful reduction in daily water use during an emergency, when you consider storing extra water for food preparation, washing hands, sanitizing surfaces and tools, and flushing toilets, that calculation starts to involve a huge amount of water. For your pets and livestock, measure their water intake on a typical day and then account for seasonality (drinking more in warmer months) when including their water needs in your overall estimate.

When considering how you will store and handle your water supply, be sure you start with clean water. If you're not sure if your water is clean, get a home kit to test your water for bacteria, lead, pesticides, nitrites, and chlorine. They're inexpensive and will tell you if your everyday water is safe to drink under normal (current) conditions.

Next, consider what you're storing your water in. Clear containers aren't as effective in preventing the growth of algae and bacteria. Opaque containers filter out more of the sun, so they keep the water cleaner and healthier. Before you put your water in the containers, clean and sterilize them with plain bleach (1 tsp bleach to 4 cups water) or an alternative product like Aquamira, then rinse with clean water.

When storing your water, keep the containers away from direct sunlight and high temperatures. A dark room is best. If you don't have an optimum place to store your water, just make sure that you rotate your supplies frequently. Don't freeze your water either—when water freezes it expands and can burst its container. And, of course, keep your water away from fuel, chemicals, and other toxic substances.

Rotate your containers periodically to ensure a safe water supply. Containers stored in a basement cold storage should be good for a few years. Clear containers exposed to light and heat will only last 3-6 months. Water that is chemically treated or purified will last longer—as long as five years if stored out of the heat and light. Water stored in a large capacity water filter shouldn't need to be rotated as long as it remains uncontaminated.

To experience firsthand what a radical reduction of water may feel like, consider embarking on a fun (well, fun for some personalities) test by conducting a "no water weekend." Before turning off the water running to your location, elicit the cooperation of those with whom you live. Keep in mind this will not be the most straightforward conversation you've ever had with your family, friends, and neighbors. There is plenty of fear wrapped up in the loss (even planned and temporary) of such a fundamental aspect of life.

While the neighbors may simply shrug and say "Good luck" when you ask them to please not allow those with whom you live to "borrow" some water over the weekend, your house-mates/flatmates may find a myriad of excuses to delay this experiment. Address these fears ahead of time, particularly with children and seniors, to discover what is at the root of surface-level complaints.

The end result of a "no water weekend" can be significant empowerment for everyone involved, who now know first-hand that they can store enough water ahead of time to live comfortably and safely. Following a few simple procedures, we can each store enough water to stay hydrated, clean, and thinking clearly during the aftermath of an emergency.

Conservation

For larger uses of water, such as laundry that you might be tempted simply to skip over during a weekend experiment, you can plan on either putting up with dirty clothes for a longer amount of time or implementing some additional planning for water conservation.

While your local hardware store may stock the classic washboard and tub, it's worth looking at a slightly higher tech—but still nonelectric—method for washing clothes. I like the pressure wash tumbling machines (e.g. the Wonder Clean or Wonder Wash brands) for getting clothes clean with zero electricity requirements and very low water requirements. The one caveat for these machines is that the water must be hot (we'll discuss alternative heating solutions in the Energy chapter). Expect your neighbors to ask about borrowing this machine!

Of course, keeping yourself clean is also important. Sponging off with fresh water can not only clean your body but also lift your spirits. If you decide to use some of your stored water for bathing, consider the purchase of a solar shower bag since you'll also likely be operating without electricity after a natural disaster. It's yet another item that is easily purchased with and shared by neighbors, as well as useful for that annual camping vacation. Be sure to recapture the water via a tarp to use elsewhere, such as your houseplants, vegetable garden, or for flushing the toilet.

One issue we quickly become aware of when there is a lack of water is sanitation. How do we dispose of our waste streams if there is no extra water with which to flush the toilets? Enter the ubiquitous five-gallon bucket. This humble device can be inexpensively transformed into a working toilet with the addition of a disposable plastic bag and—if you are feeling fancy—a fitted toilet seat for comfort. If you have access to sawdust to keep the smell in check, consider yourself extra lucky!

While several brands of disposable plastic bags will fit a five-gallon bucket, the Reliance brand includes a chemical insert that transforms the waste into a solid gel that your local sanitation department will accept in your trash. It also helps control odors, which will be needed as your sanitation department will not be running their trucks for weeks to months after a wide-scale natural disaster.

If the emergency is long term, remember that in years past, outhouses were strategically located where future fruit trees would be planted. All that manure does wonders for giving extra nutrients to growing food production plants. If you have no need for future fruit trees, you and your neighbors can still pre-identify good locations for different styles of pit latrines. Google is your friend when researching the best latrine method for your bioregion. Regardless of which style you choose, be sure to prepare for sanitizing hands. We use the Seventh Generation brand of nontoxic wipes or our outdoor sink (fed by water cisterns) that is attached to a gray water system, routing the excess water to food production beds.

One important aspect when thinking about our waste streams is the diversion of menstrual products. Keeping an emergency supply of menstrual products on hand is crucial, as noted in the appendices. Be sure to establish an agreed-upon procedure for disposal of the products after use if you need to keep them separate from other waste. When planning for an extended emergency, consider reusable, washable materials instead of disposables.

Filtration & Purification

A quick note on the difference between filtration and purification: Filtration is normally all you'd need to do with an unknown water source as any good filter removes debris and bacteria. The further step of purification will be needed after an emergency as sewage lines will likely have ruptured, introducing the possibility of viruses into your water systems. A typical filter will not eliminate viruses, thus the need for an additional purification step.

We can alleviate the cost and complexity of storing large amounts of water with the help of our neighbors. Your neighborhood can purchase a combination water filtration/purification system to share, such as a Big Berkey system (readily available online). Filters like the Big Berkey, or an inexpensive homemade version, can filter three or more gallons of water each hour. Those 75 gallons of daily water will go a long way toward helping you and your neighbors recover from a natural disaster.

Portable water filters and purifiers are also useful in an emergency. In our CERT training (Community Emergency Response Team—more on this later), we were taught to use chlorine bleach to purify water, but I prefer a less toxic alternative. Also, chlorine doesn't kill Giardia, an intestinal parasite. I like the products from Sawyer or LifeStraw to keep in Go Bags since they don't require batteries, have no moving parts, and involve no chemicals. Once I found out those companies give away a significant portion of purification products to deserving communities in developing countries, I liked them even more.

More expensive options such as UV light applicators are available, but sometimes low-tech is more dependable. Boiling the water is also an option, but it is likely an inefficient use of your heat sources in a power down scenario. If you do use boiling for purification, a water pasteurization indicator (WAPI) is a small inexpensive device that tells you when your water is safe to drink.

Relatively inexpensive treatments include potable iodine water purification tablets, but most brands leave a lousy taste in the water and are only intended for short-term or limited emergency use. They take about 30 minutes to activate and effectively neutralize Giardia and bacteria in the water. Betadine has been described as an all-purpose wonder drug by medical folks who regularly deploy to disaster recovery zones—it can be used to purify your drinking water with just 16 drops per gallon, or 4 drops per liter—but Betadine can have toxic effects on those who are sensitive (anaphylaxis), so take extra precautions. When purifying with Betadine, allow 15 minutes for clear water and 30 minutes for cloudy water, doubled if the water temperature is under 40F.

When handling your precious water supply, keep yourself as germ-free as possible by using rubber gloves when sterilizing and cleaning containers. Duct tape a medicine dropper to your bottles to prevent contaminating clean water.

One last thought. Though you'll be glad to have water during an emergency, you might not like the taste of your stored water. Bleach or other purification methods, or simply lack of oxygen, can make the water taste funny. You can re-oxygenate the water by pouring it back and forth between two containers, or add some Emergen-C or powdered drink mix for flavor. Emergen-C will also give you some valuable vitamins and help keep you hydrated.

Reclamation

But what do you do when there's no water coming out of the tap? Even if we have purification methods stored in our emergency supplies, where do we find the significant amount of water our neighborhood will require?

Many neighborhoods already have backup water supplies in place through harvesting and storing a significant amount of rainwater via barrels or cisterns. However, we live above our neighborhood's water storage tower, and thus require an electronic pump to pull the water uphill. When the electricity goes out during a winter storm, so does the water supply to our street. So we must harvest and store our own backup water supply.

At our house we use food-grade plastic cisterns and barrels for harvesting rainwater. The barrels are stored in our greenhouse as their primary function is a heat sink, painted black to leverage their high thermal mass value absorbing heat during the day and releasing it at night to keep the greenhouse temperature regulated. But they also provide an extra 250 gallons of emergency water. And as water containers are heavier than most people realize (a seven-gallon container is about 56 pounds), rain barrels and cisterns are much more manageable when sheltering in place. Use a siphon to prevent contamination during water retrieval.

Our cisterns provide a backup supply of 5000 gallons of irrigation for our permaculture food forest, as well as emergency potable water for our neighborhood. With the regular rainfall we have here in the Pacific Northwest, our gutters flow into a central pipe that refills the tanks in just 10 days! No matter what type of rain barrel or cistern you choose, you'll need one or more basic filters to keep debris from accumulating.

Remember, in an emergency, before you can drink the water you must make it potable via one or more purification (not just filtration) systems. Consider the inexpensive purchase of stabilized oxygen to add to your stored water, protecting it and extending its life before rotation is required. Chlorine dioxide is another chemical treatment option that will keep water safe for up to 5 years and does not change the taste of the water at all. It is safe to use with chlorinated municipal water to extend its shelf life.

Cisterns also come in ferro-cement and concrete for permanent underground installations but are more susceptible to cracking during an earthquake. There is much to be said for the simplicity of picking up a rain barrel at your local feed store and placing it under the gutter downspout closest to your backyard or balcony garden. Attach a hose and let gravity do its work for a free, renewable source of irrigation water to help you grow food. But if you require more water, consider cisterns.

Retrieving water from larger holding tanks can become quite the chore, particularly if the electricity that drives a pump is out. Consider backup manual pumps such as the fitness-inspired design of the Ecologics pump from New Zealand, or the classic hand siphon pump that relies on human muscle, rather than electricity, to bring up water from a barrel, well or cistern.

But can harvested rainwater be made potable? You bet. Nifty little products from companies Sawyer and LifeStraw we discussed earlier do the trick. Google it and you'll find lots of backpacking/camping gear retailers near you, as well as websites that sell this type of useful gear.

If you don't have access to your water filtration/purification setup, don't forget morning dew. These dew droplets are clean water without need of filtration or purification. Using a clean towel, sponge, or piece of clothing, mop up morning dew off tall grasses and squeeze into a container.

Here's the rule of thumb to guesstimate how much water you could harvest annually: CATCHMENT AREA (in square feet) multiplied by the AVERAGE ANNUAL RAINFALL (in feet) multiplied by 7.48 (to convert cubic feet to gallons) equals the TOTAL RAINWATER FALLING ON THAT CATCHMENT IN AN AVERAGE YEAR.

So that is CATCHMENT AREA (ft^2) x RAINFALL (ft) x 7.48 gal/ft^3 = TOTAL AVAILABLE RAINWATER (gal/year). For me, that translates into 695,640 gallons annually. Wow!

Should we lose electric power during the prime summer growing months, we can continue to water our food crops with rainwater harvested the previous spring. When discussing neighborhood pea patch locations, be sure to include the siting of a water cistern or two nearby, preferably uphill from the garden plots to avoid the need for electricity or extra muscle power to pump the water. Resist the urge to connect these larger external systems into one, which could result in cross-connection contamination. If you do want to be able to switch from one water source to another, it's well worth the money to bring in an irrigation expert with back-flow preventers.

Living Machines: Other solutions exist for neighborhoods and campus environments such as condominium complexes and schools. Islandwood, a private 255-acre outdoor learning center nestled between the forest and shore here on Bainbridge Island, uses a Living Machine to reclaim and purify campus water before reuse in landscaping and toilets.

Ben Klasky, Executive Director of Islandwood, has this to say about the Living Machine:

Ensuring a resilient ecosystem here on our campus is important to us, which is why we installed a Living Machine to process our wastewater. By processing our wastewater to the level where it can be re-used, every gallon we re-use is a gallon we don't need to purchase. Our reclaimed water is currently used for irrigating landscape plants and in the near future, our low-flush toilets.

It's a relatively low-tech way to use beneficial bacteria to replace a process that is normally quite energy intensive. Our Living Machine can produce up to 1500 gallons a day for flushing toilets and 2000 gallons a day for irrigation and our drain field.

Knowing we won't have ruptured sewer lines connected to the city grid after a major event like an earthquake gives us peace of mind. As part of our preparedness measures, we also have a 500-gallon freshwater tank and an on-site pond that we could access for emergency potable water in case of a wide-scale emergency.

Frankly, I'm not sure why more neighborhoods and campus environments don't install Living Machines as low-cost alternatives to septic systems or connecting to larger public systems, especially in more arid regions of North America. Just based on the costs we incurred 10 years ago when building ours, it would cost significantly less per family than more traditional wastewater systems.

Earthworks: Should a drought strike, as it has in recent years in much of North America, our neighborhood gardens will need to have more significant preparations in place than just a few cisterns. As we discussed in the last chapter, per-maculturalists take a different approach to food gardening than the traditional raised bed system, seeking a better way to incorporate the food beds with the land on which they reside.

Earthwork projects such as bioswales and hugelkultur are two permaculture strategies. By piling up debris such as downed limbs and tree trunks and then covering them with soil, hugelkultur provides a beneficial bed that can also help guide and retain valuable summertime rainfall.

Jennifer and David Kim installed hugelkultur beds on their 3/4-acre yard on Bainbridge Island under the guidance of permaculture designer Chuck Estin. Here's an excerpt from one of many enjoyable conversations I've had with the Kims over the years:

We were in the fortunate situation of starting from scratch with our property. Because we had to bring in heavy equipment to take out 20+ trees, we could use that same equipment to make a series of seven hugelkultur beds with the branches and stumps from the trees we took out. The beds are carefully designed to slow down the water in a zigzag path, downhill to the corner of the yard, storing water in the hugels and earth along the way.

The hugels drain to where we dug a pond (sixty thousand plus gallons) that also fills from catchment plumbed from the house gutters. [The pond filled in just 1.5 days during a record-setting couple of days of rain.]

We are hoping to irrigate from the pond in the summer. Additionally, the hugel beds are designed to hold water in the rotting wood, which will mean less need for watering during the dry periods. We planted a food forest of fruits and nuts between the hugels, so the roots can penetrate the rotting wood contained within for water and nutrients. To create the hugelkultur beds we:

1. *Dug trenches 4-feet deep and 4-feet wide.*
2. *Filled the trenches with branches/stumps.*

3. *Covered it with non-composted horse manure, obtained from a local source.*
4. *Added dirt from the pond dig-out.*
5. *And finally, covered it with an organic soil/compost mixture.*

Rather than lining the pond, for now, we tried to create a natural "gley" (a sticky waterlogged soil subsurface layer) by lining it with hay, horse manure, cardboard, dirt, and more straw on top. The hope is that it will decompose to create a watertight bottom, but we won't know until next summer if or not that will work. The alternative will be to use a rubber pond liner.

For urban dwellers, scavenging sources for water after a disaster include hot water heaters and pipes after the shutoff valves have been closed (gravity will bring the remaining water in the pipes down to the lower floors of apartment buildings). External sources like public park ponds and creeks can be accessed, but assume the water requires purification as it has likely picked up significant amounts of bacteria and chemicals.

Too Much Water

Sometimes a natural disaster will create the opposite problem: too much water. Broken water pipes in condominium complexes and single-family dwellings have caused enormous amounts of damage in the aftermath of earthquakes. Floods bring moisture to areas of our homes we never thought would see water. Hurricanes deposit massive amounts of rainwater and storm surges where we don't want them.

While we can't stop a flood or hurricane from battering our neighborhood, we can minimize the damage caused by broken water pipes. A key part of Dr. LuAnn Johnson's *Map Your Neighborhood* program is meeting with neighbors ahead of time to create a map of the water shut-off valves in the area. A bit of preplanning and having the right tools on hand can save you and your neighbors a significant amount of damage.

Rain Gardens & Swales: We can also work ahead of time to stem the potential of too much water introduced by serious storms with the installation of "rain gardens" in areas that commonly pool during heavy rains. Rain gardens are a collection of thirsty native plants arranged in a shallow ditch (often called a swale; we'll talk more about this soon) dug on contour to the land.

Not only will rain gardens help absorb excess water during emergencies, but you also will get to enjoy the beauty of the plants year round. By selecting plants appropriate to your growing zone, you can make streets more beautiful and resilient in the face of uncertain climate change. Check with your local garden supply shops for a list of appropriate rain garden plants for your bioregion.

If you happen to have a treasure like writers Carina Langstraat or Ann Lovejoy in your community, subscribe to that person's work for seasonal recommendations. Ann is one of America's best-known and widely respected garden-ing gurus with at least 18 book titles to her name (I think I own most of them) with whom I get to practice Tai Chi each week here on our island. And Carina is one of our local librarians with 23 years of design experience in landscape design. Numerous trips to Oregon, British Columbia, and California helped Carina develop a strong understanding of architectural form, hardy growth habits, delicate han-dling, and what to do with too much water!

Carina explains that two decades ago, commercial land-scapes included miles of ubiquitous otto luyken laurel and photinia planted next to long stretches of hot asphalt. Equally ubiquitous was the water, fuel, and labor necessary to hedge their merciless growth.

With the introduction of rain gardens, we've made great strides in bringing together the aesthetic with the func-tional. Native plants that used to be frowned upon are now included in public spaces because of their inherent low maintenance needs and their ability to clean our water.

Our visual aesthetic has also become more sophisticated: we've learned to recognize that natural textures and sea-sonal changes are more visually pleasing than long lines of hedges shaped with power tools.

Swales—sometimes referred to as bioswales—are shal-low ditches of any length, one to three feet in width, and

18 inches in depth. Think of it as a thin stream bed dug on the level of the land, across the contours. I've seen similar ditches—usually placed incorrectly to true water diversion/ collection—in urban and suburban yards, filled with gravel and referred to as curtain drains. Properly sited swales can divert and store water efficiently and inexpensively (compared to cisterns or ponds).

As the swale is dug, you pile the removed soil on the downside, creating a berm, and line the interior with thirsty plants, straw, gravel, or simply leave it as-is. During a heavy rainfall, water will rush downhill into the swale, hit the berm, and spread to the left and right, pausing long enough to soak into the ground.

Given how precious water is, it makes sense to try to capture and direct freshwater, even when it is coming too fast. Swales are a great mechanism for doing so and can be a fun project to complete with neighbors and friends.

Access to Clean Water

Protecting our watersheds—areas of land that capture, store, and discharge water to a common body of water—is an important part of building community resilience. When citizens act to prepare for natural disasters and self-sufficiency, we begin to understand the importance of water to our well-being.

Identifying our watersheds and working to protect them benefits our environment and also our own sustainability in terms of long-term access to water for essential activities, including drinking and growing food.

Dr. Deborah Rudnick, who holds a PhD from UC Berkley in Ecology and is the Chair of the Bainbridge Island Watershed Council, observed, "The quality and quantity of our water is vital to so many aspects of our Island, from the food we grow, to what we get out of our faucets, to the shellfish we harvest on our shorelines and the water our children play in. Keeping our watersheds clean and intact benefits us and benefits all the many animals and plants that share our island home. It is particularly important that we protect the health and levels of our aquifers, through activities including low impact development and limiting chemical use, as they are our only source of drinking water."

When you begin to do these resilience-building projects with multiple neighbors—installing a group water cistern or a shared rain garden across property lines, or purchasing a portable water filtration system to share with others on your apartment floor—you'll find significant savings in cost and time.

Clean water is a primary concern that brings emergency preppers and permaculturalists together, working side by side on positive, resilience-building projects to prepare our neighborhoods for the next earthquake, drought, flood, forest fire, or hurricane.

And be sure to remember to enjoy the side benefits of living in a more sane, beautiful, and sustainable environment as well.

In addition to the food-related books I recommended in

the previous chapter (almost all have sections on water), here are a few more titles to add to your local library check-out list:

1. *Water Storage* by Art Ludwig

2. *Basic Country Skills* by John and Martha Storey

3. *The Field Guide to Survival* series (Nature, Wilderness, City, and Suburban) by Tom Brown

Actions: water, water, everywhere...

☐ Store sufficient water for yourself/your family.

☐ Invest in water filtration and purification systems.

☐ Discuss with neighbors an investment in a cistern or other large-scale water storage.

☐ Pre-identify good locations for pit latrines in case of an emergency (hint: you can plant a fruit tree there when you are done).

☐ Identify problem areas with excessive water in the neighborhood and propose swales or rain gardens as the solution.

PORTABLE SOLAR PANELS

ROCKET STOVES

COMMUNITY SOLAR

ENERGY

"Petroleum is not the only important resource quickly depleting. Most of the peaks that are before us cannot be avoided, but there are many things we can do to navigate down and around them so as to enhance human sanity, security, and happiness. Let us do those things."

Richard Heinberg
Author, journalist, and educator

Understanding where your regional electricity is generated is an important eye-opener for many citizens, especially when you consider the many points where it may be interrupted, most of which are out of our control. Let's explore our primary uses of energy and appropriate alternatives for our homes and neighborhoods.

Sam made his way through the forest, squinting in the bright winter sun. The ice from last night's storm glistened on the ground and in the trees. The forest was beautiful. Silent. Cold.

Sam arrived at his farming partners' home and began unloading a gift from his backpack—homemade fire starters—on the front porch when Bill came around from the back of his house.

"Gorgeous morning to be without power, huh?"

"Sure is," replied Sam. "The forest pathways are slippery, but the silence is amazing. You'd think the entire island is asleep right now."

"Being in bed under several layers is not a bad strategy right now," chuckled Nani as she opened the front door. "Here, I'll trade you for these scones."

"Scones? Seriously? How in the world did you make scones with no electricity?" asked Sam.

"The wood-fired pizza oven we made last year. We warmed it up early this morning and put in a batch of scone mix to deliver to the neighbors today. These just came out," Nani explained.

Bill added, "Figured everyone would be cold and could use something warm first thing in the morning. Last time we had an ice storm like this, the power was out for 11 days!"

Sam thanked them both and left in awe of their gumption. The smell of the scones on his walk home was intoxicating.

Uses of Energy

Energy is an enormous topic that goes well beyond the scope of our neighborhoods to affect climate change and national security, but we'll keep our focus for now on how we relate to energy as individuals who are part of a neighborhood. Individuals can certainly accomplish tasks that will have a positive impact on the neighborhood as a whole. We will also look at a few group projects that require minimal technical expertise and financial outlay, and take a brief look at larger scale projects that a neighborhood can do to supplement or get completely off the electrical grid.

In the next few chapters we'll look at four primary uses of energy and the specific projects we can work on house by house, street by street. But, first, let's agree upon a simple definition of *energy*.

Rather than using a technical definition, let's think of energy as the ability to apply a small amount of X to produce a larger amount of Y. For instance, a small amount of gasoline will produce a large number of transportation miles. A small amount of wood will produce a large amount of heat in a properly insulated home. And a small amount of planning by citizens will produce a large amount of well-being in a neighborhood during an emergency, whether it is temporary or long term.

Since electricity is rather ubiquitous, we'll assume that to be our source of energy most often, but you can substitute natural gas, coal, nuclear, propane, oil, wood, wind, hydro, tidal, or solar, depending on where you live. Of course, we can list the manual efforts of humans and animals as a viable energy source as well.

Our primary uses of energy include the following:

1. **Relief from the weather.** This means warmth in the winter and cooling in the summer, depending on where you live.

2. **Household tasks.** Cooking, cleaning, and lighting up the dark hours with ease and speed are all enjoyable daily uses of energy.

3. **Communication.** This can be two-way, such as via telephone and the Internet, as well as one-way informational sources such as radio and TV. We'll discuss this in more depth in the Communication chapter.

4. **Transportation.** This includes transportation of both goods and ourselves. We'll discuss these issues later in the Transportation chapter.

Let's go through these uses to examine alternative sources of the energy we could seek in a short-term emergency. We'll include solutions that are slightly scaled up from the level of individual apartments or houses, and definitely scaled down from citywide grids.

Solutions at this scale benefit our neighborhoods by creating more resilience in our lives. With the economies of scale achieved by organizing in groups, they also help us enjoy emotional support, skills sharing, and increased security.

Weather Relief

Whether you are fighting off the damp chill of a Pacific Northwest winter or the oppressive heat of a Texas summer, energy is a crucial part of the systems in place for protection from the weather in our home and work environments. Summertime blackouts and brownouts have become common across the country due to excessive air conditioning loads. Each winter, our island loses electricity several times since most of our power lines are above ground and we are blessed with large gorgeous trees. The wind and rain often work together to blow trees onto the power lines and remind everyone just how fragile our power system is.

When the electricity goes out in the winter months, many of our heating systems become inoperable, including systems fueled by wood, oil, or propane that still require a small amount of electricity to function, such as a wood-burning fireplace's electric blower. During these short-term outages, we can see the power of strong relationships with our neighbors. Community resources such as a shared woodlot for sustainably harvested firewood or a public swimming pool for cooling off are often overlooked as viable alternatives to weather relief.

With a pause and a moment of reflection, we realize just how wealthy we are with access to these community resources. Correspondingly, I changed the definition of wealth for myself to this: three sheds of dry, split firewood to ensure winter warmth, and ability to cook without electricity for my family and neighbors during an emergency.

While I was stacking several cords of wood a few years ago, I had time to reflect on fuel sources for heat. I had just read an article from Umbra, the hipster columnist at *Grist* online. The article compared wood, electric, and gas, sharing an interesting data set from the *Consumer Guide to Home Energy Savings*. Assuming you're burning sustainably harvested wood, the trees that grow to replace the wood absorb more carbon dioxide than is created when burning it. For those with access to this renewable resource, it's worth discussing with your neighbors for purchasing and maintaining a shared set of firewood.

In rainy conditions, you can still get a good fire going by focusing your attention on truly dry wood. Start by collecting standing deadwood from underneath larger trees, particularly evergreens if you have them in your area. The living upper branches will keep the dead lower branches dry. Cut into these dead branches to find the driest inner wood. Look for trees with a wound to harvest pitch, a natural fire accelerant. Combine the two and you'll be warm soon.

It's also well worth learning how to properly burn wood to minimize environmental damage from the carcinogenic wood smoke. For a more in-depth look at the eco-ethics behind heating with wood, Dirk Thomas's *The Woodburner's Companion* details the many types of fireplaces, stoves, and strategies for use. It is my favorite book on the subject.

Summertime electrical brownouts and blackouts can move quickly from uncomfortable to life-threatening, particularly when experienced in conjunction with a natural disaster that may include a heat wave. Whether you are out in the country, in the Deep South or southwest desert, or stuck in the middle of the large metropolitan area surrounded by concrete and glass, soaring daytime temperatures without access to shade or cooling can be dangerous.

While running a large air conditioner might be beyond the capability of most electrical backup systems, having a simple fan blowing across a pan of water can lower the temperature in a room via evaporation. This is often referred to as a "swamp cooler." You can extend this emergency trick into a lifestyle choice by placing a few decorative fish bowls filled with soil and indoor water plants in front of open windows. (Visit your local nursery and ask to see the huge variety of available water plants.) As the breeze passes over your water plants, you'll be cooling your home, saving money, cleaning the air, and creating a pleasant living/working space.

A breeze is your best ally when trying to reduce heat without electricity. The sun itself creates differences in temperature, which can be used to create a breeze, providing a cooler feeling due to the wind chill effect. The breeze causes sweat to evaporate more quickly from our skin, which in turn creates a perceived skin temperature drop. On a sweltering August day in New York, this feels great!

Seeking out natural wind tunnels and wind catchers based on natural or manmade architecture is a worthwhile use of your time before natural disaster strikes. If you have young children or you are just adventurous at heart, make this a game you play, particularly on extra windy days.

On windless but sunny days, you can search for (or build your own!) solar chimneys. A solar chimney is simply a dark-colored vertical chimney (or chimney-shaped tube) that heats when struck by the sun. This creates an updraft, cooling the room at the base of the chimney as it draws the heat up and out the top of the chimney. While not often found in rural, exurban, or suburban areas, once your eye begins to look for the shape, you'll find plenty of these in urban environments.

When planning for a natural disaster, tarps (and ropes to secure them) to create shade are worth their weight in gold. Inexpensive to acquire, easy to store, portable, and useful for a variety of projects, tarps can be erected after an emergency no matter what has changed in the environment. Whether your environment has been altered by an earthquake or tsunami, tarps are crucial for removing the relentless sun during the warmer months to provide weather relief without electricity for yourself and your neighbors.

Household Uses

North Americans have long enjoyed an uninterrupted energy in their homes for yard work, cooking, cleaning, and lighting up the night. It is possible to perform each of these tasks without power during a short-term emergency, but eating energy bars and reading by candlelight will only get you so far.

It's in the home and with our immediate neighbors that we remember our original source of energy: ourselves. Extra human power is required when our laborsaving devices don't have the required electricity to run, and, as our grandparents would tell us, sharing the work among many hands makes for light work. Relying solely on human power also challenges us to create mechanical energy-producing methods, like bicycling.

Pedal power is one of the primary topics you'll find in the entertaining and inspiring book by Tamara Dean, *The Human Powered Home: Choosing Muscles Over Motors.* Tamara's book is full of diagrams and plans to build a variety of laborsaving devices... that still require a bit more labor than just plugging it into a wall socket! From a pedal-powered laptop to treadle-powered washing machine, this book is a gem for do-it-yourself enthusiasts.

Yard Maintenance: We maintain our lawn and pasture with a combination of scythe, push mower, and small electric mower. All of these are infinitely more enjoyable to use than the obnoxiously loud and environmentally damaging gas-powered mower we replaced. With my old DR Power pasture mower, I dreaded the "wasted" Saturdays I would have to spend cutting pathways in the tall grass while drowning in fumes, noise, and unnatural vibrations. I was more than happy to trade it in for a silent scythe and, surprisingly, when I take into account maintenance hours formerly devoted to the engine, my cutting times stayed the same.

Tools such as a scythe and alternatives mowers are ideal for sharing among neighbors since they are not needed daily. In addition to spreading the costs and maintenance across several neighbors, the learned techniques with the scythe can be shared as well. The basic technique is a full-bodied twist with a slight springing up in the legs. Holding the scythe gently by its two handles, draw the blade from right to left as you progress through the area you are cutting. Your arms and shoulders stay relaxed; it's your core twisting motion that is creating the energy transfer down to the blade. While not exhausting or too strenuous, you will save money by not needing to go to the gym on the days you use the scythe. We have four scythes for our family of four, sized all the way down to one appropriate for our elementary age child, so we can work together.

As with all your hand tools, from scythes to shovels, it's well worth your time to keep the blades and edges sharp. You'll dig that hole twice as fast with a sharp-edged shovel recently tuned up with a hard file, and you'll get through your cutting chores faster if you stop from time to time to re-sharpen your scythe's blade with a whetstone. My ratio is to stop for one minute of sharpening after about 15 minutes of cutting. If you want to join me in full geekiness, find a copy of David Tresemer's excellent *The Scythe Book*.

While we're talking about lawns, consider bucking the illogical trend of maintaining a lawn at all. Consider converting some (or all!) of it into food production. If you are so inclined, pick up a copy of *Food Not Lawns* by Heather Jo Flores at your local library. It's an inspiring read centered on permaculture, and I love the book's subtitle: "How to turn your yard into a garden and your neighborhood into a community."

Cooking and Cleaning: Heating water on a cook stove does require extra time and elbow grease since it is most commonly fueled by wood. But on the flip side, cook stove installations do not need to be permanent nor expensive. Do a quick search on YouTube for "rocket stoves" and you'll find a plethora of designs that require very little time and expense to create but can boil large amounts of hot water with very little wood fuel. The stoves we've built literally take twigs—not large pieces of firewood—to produce significant amounts of heat for cooking and boiling water.

Although this tool might only be brought out when the electricity has been cut, keep in mind that modern gas and electric cooking stoves are usually less energy inefficient than cooking directly with a wood fire. Certainly, our modern cooking stoves are more practical and produce significantly less indoor pollution than open fires. But you'll be pleasantly surprised how easy, educational, and fun biomass stoves can be to bring out for a weekend barbeque experience with friends!

You can combine rocket stoves with non-electric slow-cookers, such as the Wonderbag, to widen your cooking abilities even more. Products like these are simple insulated pouches that continue to slow-cook the ingredients in your pot after the water is brought to a boil. Wonderbag is my favorite among these types of products as they donate a bag to an African family for each one you purchase.

While it is common sense, it's worth mentioning that biomass stoves should only be used outdoors in well-ventilated areas. As you involve children from the neighborhood in these projects, ensure they understand the importance of this as well.

Increasing Energy Efficiency

One of the largest energy uses in most living quarters is hot water. If your neighborhood has the foresight to build a biomass cook stove (a great thing to ask about during your Map Your Neighborhood meeting), during an emergency you can use it to heat water for cleaning clothes and dishes.

To see a live, working, beautiful model of what cooking and cleaning look like at the neighborhood level—with or without electricity—finagle yourself an invitation to dinner at the closest intentional community or co-housing community. This is a viable and attractive model to replicate in low- or no-power scenarios. In addition to lowering the workload per person, sharing meals also foster increased emotional support and communication, which will be crucial in the aftermath of a wide-scale natural disaster. Perhaps the sexiest efficiency project you can take on is installing solar panel arrays on your roof. That's right, I said solar is sexy! But don't let your long-term dream of solar panels stand in the way of much simpler projects you can undertake in the short-term. I am guilty of having spent months thinking about solar panels before realizing I had not replaced a single light bulb with more energy efficient versions, nor had I taken the time to seal up excessive air leaks in my own home.

The best energy investment you can make is improving your existing dwelling with insulation. It's a relatively inexpensive project, requiring one year (or less) in payback, and is a great example of the power of group purchases. The next time your neighbors get together for a meeting, ask if anyone else is interested in saving money on utility bills and making their homes more comfortable. Most folks will give an enthusiastic "yes."

Moving one level up from an individual neighborhood, bioregional differences can be leveraged for small-scale energy capture and storage. Here in the northwest, organizations like Solar Washington have successfully organized many group purchases from citizens. And your local land-based nonprofits can be a part of this as well, universities being a prime example.

The University of California, San Diego, sources a significant amount of their energy from solar panels. On the other coast, Stockton College of New Jersey is harvesting offshore wind in the Atlantic. Carleton College in Northfield, Minnesota, is pulling almost half of its energy needs from its own wind farm. The learning and success happening on our local college campuses can apply directly to towns and larger neighborhoods in those same bioregions.

Attitude Adjustment

As we seek alternative energy sources during short-term emergencies, we gain understanding and new ideas about permanent ways to scale back from fossil fuels. But this requires a significant attitude adjustment. Some believe access to oil and natural gas to be a "right," but they are sadly mistaken. We've come to expect low gasoline and oil prices for the transportation of goods and people without thinking through the true cost of the fuel or what we will do when it becomes unaffordable.

We've come to expect ubiquitous electricity for instant communications, easy cleaning, fast cooking, lighting the darkness, and relief from the weather. When a natural disaster interrupts the flow of that electricity to our homes and workplaces, we're given a glimpse of what we need to prepare for in the coming Long Emergency, when plentiful oil disappears, creating scarcities in everything from transportation to food.

Some countries are making serious progress in this area, such as Scotland. During the summer of 2016, Scotland produced 106 percent of its electrical needs by wind for an entire day. Think about that for a moment. Even with the caveats that they had strong winds that particular day and low demand for electricity, that is still a significant milestone for a country to reach on its journey away from fossil fuel dependence. Unfortunately for the US, this is not something we can assume our federal or state governments will fix in a timely manner.

But good news! Our military, with its enormous resources, has turned its attention to the problem. Two interesting new terms to me that surfaced in the last few years are climate patriots and environmental security. Climate Patriots is a short video you can find on YouTube and elsewhere that provides a military perspective on energy, climate change, and American national security. It's backed by The Pew Project on National Security, Energy and Climate, which conducted a series of interviews with former military leaders to discuss the challenges posed to the U.S. armed forces due to the impacts of climate change and our energy posture.

The private sector is also coming around with a significant attitude adjustment. According to Bloomberg, more Americans now work in solar than in oil, gas, or coal (we're talking about the extractive industries themselves, not the local gas station attendant). The International Renewable Energy Agency (IRENA) reported 2015 solar industry employment at approximately 208,000 while the US Bureau of Statistics reported employment in oil and gas at 185,000 and 190,000 in coal that same year. With coal and natural gas quickly becoming less cost competitive to alternatives like wind and solar, we can expect this employment trend to continue, which is great news.

I'll admit that as a social entrepreneur, I'm more than a bit biased, believing massive systemic change comes best from the private sector. Just one energy/transportation example to demonstrate my point: the electric car company Tesla has only made money in one quarter so far, as they are spending enormous sums on R&D. But in a single quarter of 2016, they made more profit ($22 million) than the entire US oil industry. In fact, in that same year, the US oil industry lost $67 billion and cut 100,000 jobs according to the US Energy Information Administration (EIA). Ouch.

Citizens can also get involved in the mindset shift by creating alternative energy systems in their neighborhoods to supplement or backup our grid-tied systems. This provides much-needed relief during a wide-scale emergency like an earthquake or hurricane. And, who knows, once we create these alternative systems, perhaps we'll decide we like the slower, more deliberate, and (potentially) more enjoyable pace of life necessitated in low-power situations.

One solution we've not yet tried on our island but I'm currently fascinated by is portable/retractable solar panels. One example appropriate at the neighborhood scale is Roll-Array from Renovagen. Imagine a flexible carpet made of photovoltaic panels that rolls out from a trailer small enough to be hauled around by a typical SUV. Whenever and wherever you need portable power, you unroll the PV panels to create an instant microgrid via the batteries and inverters housed in the trailer. The entire system can be set up in minutes with just a couple of people to generate enough electricity for several streets or a field medical treatment area set up to handle the wounded after a large emergency. Amazing.

One more aspect of attitude to be considered is how we view technology. Since much of my career has been in high tech, I've thought about this concept of "technology as savior" for years. While companies like Renovagen and Tesla are making amazing progress, I regularly have conversations with otherwise deep-thinking individuals who dismiss immense problems such as climate change with the wave of a hand. They state, "Oh, some high-tech genius will solve that." When I try to explain that Moore's Law is not a useful answer for how we might deal with an increase of climate-induced natural disasters nor the unintended consequences of our "solutions," it usually falls on deaf ears. But I'm not alone in making this argument.

John Perkins is the best-selling author of *Confessions of an Economic Hitman* among many other books. He's also one of my mentors and most trusted friends. When discussing this topic, John reminded me, "Technology will not get us out of this. It is good to recall that in my grandmother's day, cars were hailed as the solution to terrible pollution and food shortages. Horse manure was inundating our cities; NYC's East River was choked with the stuff every winter when it was plowed—along with snow—into the river. And inordinate amounts of farmlands surrounding major cities were devoted solely to growing horse food! Solar, wind, and related alternatives may offer limited short-term solutions to fossil fuels, but if taken to the huge scales currently required, they will have negative impacts (like the car) as yet undetermined."

Peak Everything

For several of these energy sources, we are near, at, or past peak production, which is a significant part of what is leading us into the Long Emergency. While this is still controversial thinking for some, consider the research of the majority of the world's scientists and deep-thinkers on the topic of peak production of oil, including NASA scientist James Hansen and Bill Gates (look up his TED Talk).

If this particular topic strikes a passion point for you, you'll likely find the Transition Town movement fascinating (visit transitionus.org for North American readers). It takes a holistic but energy-centric approach to building resilience into towns. I've gone through their training and found it to be excellent. Our own local efforts through Sustainable Bainbridge programs match well with the tenets of the Transition Town movement.

I spoke at length with my friend and neighbor Hilary Franz, Washington State Lands Commissioner and Executive Director of Futurewise in Seattle, about this topic of energy. As she's been involved with local politics for much of her career, she described how much of the leadership for energy independence in the Pacific Northwest has come from island communities.

Our area's islands are more vulnerable to significant economic and environmental pressures, and their smaller population size makes movement at the political level easier. Hilary spoke about the benefit to smaller towns of thinking big while implementing rapid small-scale change in local leadership to build an engaged community. This also works at the neighborhood level in larger metropolitan areas, particularly municipalities that allocate budget based on neighborhood density.

By beginning with streets and neighborhoods—rather than federal/state committees—it is easier to learn what matters to citizens on a daily basis, whether it is environmental sustainability or economic survival. Former Speaker of the House, Tip O'Neill, was spot-on when he said: "All politics is local."

Hilary went on, "We have the technologies to restructure the nation's energy economy and reduce greenhouse gas emissions. Almost everything we need to do to move the energy economy has already been done in one or more communities."

We talked about other island communities and their need for a more secure approach to meeting their own energy needs. Samso is a small island in Denmark with 4,000 inhabitants that produces more energy from renewable resources than it consumes. The wind provides 100 percent of Samso's electricity needs. Nearby in Iceland—a country with a population the size of a small US city of 300,000 citizens—they have almost eliminated the use of coal for heating, relying instead on geothermal. Back here in the States, Martha's Vineyard in Massachusetts has a community-owned energy cooperative, Vineyard Power. A membership buys a share in the cooperative, and any profits the cooperative makes will return to the shareholders, rather than a third-party utility.

Hilary and I also talked about small- to medium-sized townships pursuing strategies in other bioregions to become more energy independent and reduce carbon footprints. She told me about towns in Michigan and Maine that have serious winters to think about.

The city of Ann Arbor, Michigan, has an aggressive energy efficiency program that includes upgrading municipal buildings, converting to LED streetlights, and installation of a biogas facility, a small hydropower facility, and a solar power facility. In Vinalhaven, a rural community in Penobscot Bay, Maine, they recently completed work on three land-based wind turbines that provide enough energy for the entire island in the summer and a surplus that will return benefits to cooperative members in the winter.

Hilary wrapped up our conversation with comments on our own island's long-term initiatives, "Bainbridge Island has taken similar steps to set and achieve clean energy goals, with a goal of increasing energy efficiency in homes, installing larger scale renewable energy systems like the solar thermal system in the park district's aquatic center, and solar systems in all of its schools and municipal buildings. The community is looking at larger renewable energy installations in the future like district energy systems fueled by a large amount of biomass on the island."

Rethinking Our Energy

I encourage you to bring an open mind to any discussion about energy as it is at the core of many of the problems we face in emergencies, whether they are long or short. The always-brilliant author Seth Godin makes a particularly compelling argument (with graphics) for citizens to at least recognize that we've all been marketed to by various energy groups and look at the data through a different lens for a moment.

death rate per watts produced

Understanding where your regional electricity is generated is an important eye-opener for many citizens. For instance, in the Pacific Northwest, where an increasing amount of energy is created by wind and water, a significant source is still created by burning coal at the Colstrip Generating Facility in Montana. Award-winning photographer David T. Hanson gives a compelling talk and slideshow, describing the environmental and societal impacts of this facility. You can find his powerful images with the accompanying text at davidthanson.net.

Whether or not you believe we should continue burning coal, the fact that electricity for our towns is often generated far away and therefore requires long transportation lines is cause for concern when we're thinking about emergencies. Creating decentralized, local backup solutions pertinent to their bioregions builds resilience into our towns and neighborhoods, and it helps us move one step closer to a more sustainable environmental solution.

The conversion at Samso to renewable energy systems occurred at just the right time: an economic downturn. Samso citizens saw the development of wind energy generating $8 million in revenue per annum through the export of energy and pursued it partially because of the return on investment. Locally to me, our island's energy efficiency program was created as an effort to address a depressed construction industry, higher-than-average residential energy bills, and the desire to avoid a new multimillion-dollar substation that sparked controversial NIMBY (not in my backyard) debates.

Perhaps the leading candidate in North America for making the most progressive and aggressive commitment to clean energy is Burlington, Vermont, with its 42,000 citizens. Starting back in the 1980s with a little-known leader at the time—Bernie Sanders—Burlington's citizens set out on a path towards sustainability. The area had been attracting an educated, back-to-the-land, socially conscious demographic of citizens for over a decade, which inadvertently laid the groundwork for citizens' personal ethos to bubble up into public policy.

With Sanders leading the way as mayor, widespread municipal initiatives were created, focusing first on energy, recycling (one of the first in the nation), and incubating local businesses (again, one of the first efforts in the nation). Their primary energy project was a biomass plant converting an excess of local wood to electricity. As pioneers in the area, they wrote their own sustainable forestry practice guidelines, which are still in effect today.

Peter Clavelle replaced Sanders as mayor and continued their focus on energy into the 1990s. He shepherded an $11+ million bond through the approval process for energy efficiency improvements in both residential and commercial areas. On a wider scale, Clavelle encouraged the creation of Burlington's Legacy Plan, a citizen-led overarching plan for continued community sustainability. The Legacy Plan included sections on transportation, development, food security, and energy-related initiatives such as mandatory recycling, radically lowered energy consumption, and a serious investment in renewable power.

At the center of this renewable power sits the 7.5-megawatt Winooski One hydroelectric plant, constructed in 1994. Developed privately, it was purchased by citizens in recent years with a $12 million bond, making Burlington the nation's first 100 percent renewable energy city. The current mayor, Miro Weinberger, commented: "It's really pushed us to think hard and big about where we go from here. That's when we started looking at what net zero would look like." *Net zero* refers to a town that generates as much energy as it consumes, including electricity, heat, and transportation. We'll talk more about transportation later in the book.

While the communities we've discussed appear to be doing something extraordinary or alternative, they are actually just making smart investments in their future. As we discussed with the permaculture principles, these investments are simply a culmination of many small steps. Small steps that can be begun today in your community!

These communities—and their civic and citizen leaders—are not waiting for state or federal action. They recognize that we've simply run out of time to wait. The shared hope among these community leaders is that other cities will mirror their ideas, applying them to their own towns. This patchwork of communities pursuing energy independence can transform our nation's energy economy, one town at a time.

Actions: moving towards sustainable solutions:

☐ Unless you live on the equator, collect and keep a sufficient stack of firewood each season. Consider setting aside more for your neighbors if you have room.

☐ Set up (or make ready the materials to set up) a swamp cooler, solar chimney, and rocket stove. These are fun projects to do with kids, too!

☐ Purchase tarps and ropes. "Buy Nothing" online groups and garage sales are great places to find items like these for cheap.

☐ Explore neighborhood solar and other off-grid power generation alternatives.

TENTS IN THE PARK

GO BAGS.

COMMUNITY CENTERS

SHELTER

"The 20th century single-family suburban home alienated from the surrounding landscape may soon be obsolete. The norms for housing in the coming era of energy austerity will have to be much more traditional and integral with their surroundings. Since we will have to grow more of our food close to home, the land will be valued more for agriculture than for commuter houses."

James Howard Kunstler
Author and social critic

"Gimme Shelter" is more than a classic song by the Rolling Stones. It's a call for the basic human need of protection from the elements and a source of physical and emotional security. Although we can live for three days without water and three weeks without food (albeit uncomfortably), we may only survive three hours without shelter in severe weather.

Amy walked into the open garage—dripping wet—accompanied by two seemingly-happy dogs of equal wetness.

"We finally got that rusted cutoff valve off," she announced to the small group of neighbors gathered in the darkness. "Thank goodness we had channel locks. It took two of us ten minutes working on it before the water finally stopped!"

The earthquake had interrupted the dinner hour for the greater Seattle region. Although everyone was upset, injuries were minor and Amy's neighbors had been successfully working their way down their Map Your Neighborhood checklist for the last twenty minutes. With the electricity out, flashlights and headlamps provided the needed illumination.

It was November and the near-constant drizzle of rain had returned to the Pacific Northwest after a long and beautiful summer. As the neighbors assembled at their pre-designated gathering point, a stash of dry towels was produced and warm clothing pulled from closets in homes that were still accessible.

Amy's neighbor, Paul, updated her as he toweled off one of the dogs: "Everyone had posted OK signs on their front doors except the Pfiefer family. But they responded when we yelled in through the broken front windows. Everyone is OK. They were just frazzled."

"Good," replied Amy. She then turned to the group, "Is everyone dry and warm? Yes? Great, then let's see what our next step is." They returned their attention to the handful of Map Your Neighborhood checklists that were still readable despite the rain.

In the winter, we must be able to maintain our body's core temperature via shelter to stave off hypothermia, and in the summer heat, we need to find relief from the sun's dehydrating rays. Shelter helps us accomplish both.

What shelter doesn't need to be is luxuriously spacious. In the context of emergency preparedness, shelter is closer to our concept of camping. The primary requirements of shelter after an emergency are (1) protection from weather—particularly cold, wind, rain, and penetrating sun—and (2) a source of heat.

When You Need to Go

In certain emergencies, your home might be uninhabitable for a short—or long—period of time. Whether you're going to a neighborhood care center or shelter, or breaking out the camping gear, you'll want to be prepared for the time you'll be away from home.

Go Bags: Go Bags are commonly kept by frequent business travelers or military folks who need to travel at a moment's notice. A Go Bag is simply a piece of luggage containing all the essentials you need for a few days. It's easy to create or modify these to be appropriate for preparedness. Creating one is as simple as organizing that collection of camping gear you have and staging the bag(s) near your vehicle or your building's primary exit.

Wherever you go to escape an emergency, your Go Bags

will provide you with a sense of calm readiness. We have a Go Bag for each member of our family, including the animals. The same basics of a prepared home apply to the contents of a complete Go Bag: a portable shelter (tent or tarp), a heat source, food, water, and a means of communication. You'll find a complete list of suggested items to include in your Go Bag in the appendix, but two items are worth elevating here for your attention: socks and shirts.

Ask any homeless shelter director what their most requested item is and you'll hear one consistent answer: socks. In your Go Bag, be sure to include multiple pairs of hiking socks (thicker and warmer than regular socks) in a freezer grade Ziploc bag so if you and or your feet get wet, you'll have dry socks to change into.

If there is a possibility of going to an emergency shelter, consider purchasing oversized tee shirts for every family member, all in the same blazing bright color, with your family's last name printed on the back. Yes, you will look goofy. But no, you won't care, because you'll be able to find each other quickly, even in a large shelter or outdoor tented area, and the visuals will provide extra reassurance to small children since they will be able to quickly spot their guardians. Use oversized shirts so you can put them on over warm clothes if needed.

If you are a pet owner, create a separate Go Bag for each animal you might take with you, which from our micro-farm is a German Shepard and two barn cats. We would not attempt to bring the chickens along!

A pet's Go Bag should contain a sturdy leash, harness and/or collar with identification tags, medications, a collapsible water bowl, and their normal food. For smaller animals or animals not known for being responsive to voice commands (looking at you, felines!), consider keeping an animal carrier with your Go Bags. More details and suggestions for pet Go Bags can be found in the appendix.

I recently modified my own Go Bag to reflect my additional duties as a CERT (Community Emergency Response Team) member to include medical triage and search and rescue. While we'll cover this in more depth later, please consider this quick sales pitch for CERT: after you have your personal preparations complete, CERT (or any number of similarly named organizations) is well worth looking into as your own "Step 10." Remember, Step 10 is about sharing your unique skills and expertise with others after you complete the first nine steps of Map Your Neighborhood in the aftermath of an emergency. There are several international versions of CERT as well (more on this later in the Personal Training chapter).

Get Home Bags: Get Home Bags are smaller versions of Go Bags for commuters. Years ago when I worked at Microsoft, my workplace was on the east side of Seattle. To get back to Bainbridge Island, I'd need to find my way across a floating bridge to downtown Seattle, then across the Puget Sound to Bainbridge. That would be quite a journey if highways were blocked, bridges were down, and ferry docks had been destroyed.

Think through your own daily commute and what specific challenges you may face returning home by foot. Your Get

Home Bag is where you keep specific supplies to help you find your way back home after a major disaster. Different than your Go Bag, the sole focus of your Get Home Bag is to complete that one journey back to your loved ones. While the contents will vary based on the geographic aspects of your specific commute, suggestions for inclusions in your Get Home Bag are in the appendix.

One item for urban environments that I'll call attention to here is the inexpensive (<USD$10) sillcock key. This small tool allows you access to the water system of most commercial buildings from the outside of the building. Even in a power down situation, the building will have enough internal pressure to push water out to refill your bottle and give you the energy to keep going. YouTube has plenty of short videos on how to find these valves on the exterior of buildings and how to use the key to open them.

Heat Sources Away from Home: We've already touched on the more permanent aspects of heating sources for shelter as they relate to energy. But those permanent heating sources are not much use when you need to leave that shelter behind. When you're away from home, your primary source of heat will be... yourself!

We've already discussed the camp stove's cousin, the easy-to-make biomass stove. A camp stove isn't actually meant to warm the air around you, but rather to warm the food and beverages that will go a long way towards keeping your spirits high, your brain functioning well, and your body producing its own heat. The cost and maintenance of a shared camp stove and fuel among neighbors is quite low, and high-quality choices for camp stoves abound at your local retailers. Some stoves, like the Biolite, don't even require fuel canisters to be kept on hand—like a rocket stove, you simply feed it small dry twigs for fuel.

Our bodies themselves are excellent heat sources when proper insulation is applied. Whether that is a Mylar blanket (or better yet a Heat Sheet or survival bag), newspapers stuffed inside clothing, proper outdoor apparel, a full survival or mummy sleeping bag, or a properly sized tent, our bodies can produce a surprising amount of heat with a thoughtful mix of insulation and shelter. The same items you might use when camping outside in the winter are what you will stock in your Go Bags.

An aside about Mylar. While the ubiquitous little silver Mylar blankets are inexpensive and take up very little room in a pack, there are far superior products to provide warmth when you really need it, such as SOL Products' heat-reflective blankets and survival bags. There is also a classification of emergency bags that are heavier than Mylar but lighter than full "mummy" sleeping bags you might get from REI, The North Face, or Wiggy's. Look up Titan Survival to see examples of these mid-range survival bags.

Shelter in Place

Some emergencies, such as hurricanes, can be anticipated, giving people ample time for escape. Other emergencies force us to shelter-in-place or stay put for a given number of hours, days, or weeks, until the emergency passes. A chemical spill on the nearby highway will force you indoors for a number of hours or days. A major earthquake will force you to stay in your home area for weeks or months due to destroyed highways, airports, and other key infrastructure. With that in mind, any precautions that you can take for your own home, like creating a "safe room," can be extended to neighbors as well as you shelter in place together.

There are basic retrofit projects applicable to many homes to ensure a safer, more expedient recovery from a natural disaster. If you have access to your hot water tank, ensure it has an earthquake strap. All tall furniture (e.g. bookcases) should be strapped to studs in the walls behind them. Consider adding safety catches on your higher kitchen cabinets to keep the dishes contained.

Scan each room of your dwelling to see what heavy objects could be moved lower, whether that is in your pantry or on bookshelves. Relocate any heavy or glass-lined picture frames away from your sleeping areas. Your local hardware store has relatively inexpensive kits for completing these basic safety retrofit projects.

Add an annual reminder to check your smoke alarms as well as turn over all fire extinguishers and give them a gentle knock with a rubber mallet. This dislodges the internal chemicals that have settled and will extend the life of your extinguisher.

The Safe Room: The existing shells of our homes are a decent first layer barrier for protection against airborne chemical agents that might be released during a chemical truck spill on the highway, or when a tornado or earthquake damages a nearby industrial area. A safe room adds a significantly higher degree of safety to that outer shell your home provides. Choose an easily accessed room that can be quickly sealed to store enough food, water, comfort, and sanitary supplies to protect you and your loved ones for at least one full day. Experts tell us that in those emergencies that require a safe room, we'll usually be able to emerge within a few hours, however, having extra supplies on hand means you can take in more neighbors or visitors who happen to be nearby.

To prepare a safe room, store enough thick plastic sheeting and duct tape to cover all vents, doors, and windows (pre-cut and label these pieces if you want to get really ambitious). If at all possible, choose a room with running water and/or a toilet as your short-term refuge. This also gives you ample water to dampen a set of towels to ensure a snug seal under the doors and windows.

Include a two-way communication device such as a cell phone and charging cord in your safe room, as well as a one-way communication device such as a radio or TV so you have access to outside information. Consider including a few comfort items as well, such as a deck of playing cards or your children's favorite book series. It will help pass the time and keep everyone calm.

Helpful Landscaping

Let's shift our attention to the outside of our structures now. As recent extreme weather events have become commonplace due to climate change, professionals now consider resilience when designing both the buildings in which we work and live, as well as the landscapes that surrounds them. In cities around the world, designers are seeking to work with nature instead of against it. Rather than build in avalanche and landslide-prone areas, city architects are now designating those areas as open space parks. For example, a recently installed park in Singapore is located in one of the city's floodplains. Bishan-Ang Mo Kio Park's design mitigates frequent flooding from the nearby river to divert the water away from the city.

As we discussed in the water chapter, rain gardens apply the same concept on a smaller scale to our homes and neighborhoods. Similarly, when combatting heat gain from harsh summer sunshine (particularly in the South), trees can offer significant help to our shelters in keeping us cool. Those same sturdy trees may fair better during a natural disaster than the nearby dwellings, thus retaining their ability to help us stay cool and calm while we shelter in place during a hot summer.

This even works in larger cities, notorious for the extra heat generated by buildings and concrete. One only has to take a brief stroll from the core of New York City into the famous Central Park to notice an immediate and significant drop in temperature, right there in the heart of one of our largest cities. Proper siting of trees and buildings not only helps with shading for summertime heat relief, it also influences the wind. Neighborhood planners in Stuttgart, Germany keep their streets cooler in the summer by orienting buildings to better leverage the wind to offer cooling breezes.

These design practices can be incorporated into neighborhoods to create passive microclimates conducive to growing food, providing relief from extreme weather, and encouraging interactions between neighbors. Let's talk a bit more about the importance of those neighborly interactions when it comes to shelter.

Reunification

One of the lessons for emergency professionals learned from the Christchurch earthquake is the importance of families staying together; every family should have a reunification plan should a natural disaster occur when family members are scattered (please see template in Appendix D).

Having an out-of-area contact person is useful for coordination when local communication networks become overloaded. Since my family lives on an island in the Pacific Northwest, we have a three-part reunification plan: (1) an agreed-upon out-of-area contact person in the Midwest; (2) an out-of-region reunification spot if we need to find each other outside of the greater Seattle area; and (3) local friends on both sides of the Puget Sound where we can temporarily find shelter.

Should we find ourselves off the island without our children, we have confidence that our friends, neighbors and the Map Your Neighborhood game plan would provide temporary care for our children. A strong community provides a significant amount of peace and confidence regarding the care of special populations like young children and elders. That community is grounded in our neighborhoods.

Think through your own situation and discuss it with your loved ones. Even if you are not dealing with bodies of oceanic water separating you from each other, developing a reunification plan and ensuring each family member is aware of the details is an important step in your larger plan for shelter after a natural disaster.

If the disaster is widespread and significant, we'll all find ourselves hosting others (or being hosted) for weeks to months as damage is being repaired. Frequent, honest communication among new housemates about expectations and changing needs is of utmost importance during these stressful times. During this period of significant transition for potentially an entire bioregion, daily and weekly check-in conversations among folks temporarily living together will strengthen relationships rather than fray them.

In the economy of the last decade or so, it's not unusual to have friends lose their homes. Even without a disaster, you may be called upon to host neighbors and friends. Over the years, we've had various families live with us and have learned some valuable co-housing lessons—centered mostly on communication—that will benefit us should we find ourselves living in someone else's home after an emergency. You might consider doing the same; opening your home to those in need now. Each person will learn resilient communication strategies to benefit you in the future.

Self-Sufficiency vs. Resilience

I spoke with Matthew Stein, author of *When Technology Fails,* about the wisdom of moving from a self-sufficiency attitude ("I just need my own skills and my own stuff") to a more resilient perspective of relying on trusted folks around you to navigate short and long-term emergencies.

Matt explained, "No one person can possibly cover 100 percent of their needs in a long-term emergency, particularly as population increases and natural resources decrease. We must work together, particularly as our technology begins to fail us. Good old-fashioned people power—not the latest gadget or gear—is the key to successful grassroots efforts to thrive in the future. I find hope in the permaculture and Transition Town movements. Throughout human history, great changes have followed actions that began with individuals, households, and communities."

So we recognize that working with our neighbors is a better approach than going solo, but isn't that going to create more "stuff" we need to store for emergencies? How does assembling and storing preparedness gear (alongside stores of water and food) reconcile with living a more sustainable lifestyle with a smaller footprint, less debt, and more happiness? Is it possible to reconcile the tension between a desire to be and feel prepared (which for most folks equals more gear) and a desire for a streamlined, smoother, "go light" experience in life?

I've struggled with these questions for over a decade, ever since reading Ray Jardine's *Lightweight Backpacking* book. Jardine had a huge influence on my family paring down our gear (and the rest of our stuff) years ago. I posed those questions to minimalist Joshua Becker of the *Becoming Minimalist* blog.

Here's what Joshua told me:

These are great questions. In fact, one of the greatest problems relative to overconsumption in our society today is the misplaced search for security and/or preparedness. The pursuit of security is common among all of us. We've just been looking for it in all the wrong places.

Too many of us believe security can be adequately found in possessions. Now there is a degree of truth to that statement. Certainly, food and water and clothing and shelter are essential for survival. But the list of possessions that we truly need is quite minimal.

Instead, we have confused needs with wants and security with luxury. As a result, many of us pursue and collect large stockpiles of possessions in the name of security or happiness. We work long hours to purchase them. We build bigger houses to store them. And we spend more energy maintaining them. The burden of accumulating and maintaining slowly becomes the main focus of our lives.

Meanwhile, we lose community, freedom, happiness, and

passion. We exchange some of the most basic elements of life for more possessions. Our search for security and life and joy is essential to being human. We just need to start looking for it in the right places.

Enjoying the Benefits of Preparedness Now

While we seek to keep our group purchases of supplies with neighbors in moderation, we can specifically make a point of focusing on the most resilient aspect of all: the strong relationships that will develop from more communication and group projects with those who live around us. Like many related sustainability or "green" group initiatives, resilience projects we take on with our neighbors will encourage us to enjoy the benefits of preparedness now.

As David Holmgren discusses in his *Endurance of Suburbia* talks, the typical American neighborhood can be retrofitted by wise citizens—not governments—to increase its resilience. If we place enough solar panels on homes, we can have energy-independent neighborhoods. If we create enough stormwater runoff diversions from our paved streets into cleaning basins, we can have water security for hundreds of neighbors at a time. These "green" projects also provide significant resources in times of emergency as backup systems.

One example would be improving the insulation in our dwellings. Our homes will be better equipped to provide adequate shelter after an emergency if we take a few steps now toward improving their energy efficiency. As we discussed in the energy chapter, a group purchase of insulation is a great place to start the conversation with neighbors. Many municipalities and states are now offering incentives to do these projects, which end up saving you money as soon as you complete them. You'll see your utility bills drop the first month after installation.

A second example would be dealing with fires. Fires not only create a second wave of injuries after a natural disaster, they can strike at any time. A simple step that can be taken now is the purchase (and maintenance) of fire extinguishers that are appropriate for our homes. Step six in the MYN pamphlet reminds us to set our unused fire extinguishers outside our front doors, on the sidewalks or in the central hallways of shared spaces, in clear view of the neighbors. Should a fire start in one home on your street, the combined set of extinguishers from the rest of your neighbors will prove useful.

One item we've added to our set of MYN materials stored under each bed is a fire mask (sometimes called oxygen hoods). These relatively inexpensive items are cheap insurance to ensure you have enough clean oxygen to retrieve your loved ones and exit the building in case of a fire. The Go Time Gear brand of fire escape mask gives you 60 minutes to get out of the toxic environment.

Making small individual preparations now—like purchasing and maintaining fire extinguishers and oxygen hoods—will provide shared benefits for you and your neighbors later. John Schelling, the Earthquake/Tsunami/

Volcano Program Manager for the Washington Emergency Management Division, drove home this point in a conversation we had about better preparing where we live. We discussed instances ranging from single-family dwellings to multifamily residential community and even entire subdivisions.

John spoke of greatly enhancing our community resilience by increasing the ability of families and neighborhoods to bounce back more quickly following a natural disaster: "Spending time in a crowded disaster shelter with few creature comforts is not what most people would consider ideal, especially for weeks or months after a big disaster like an earthquake or tsunami. A key component of disaster preparedness and community resilience is ensuring that our homes are structurally safe enough to stay in, even if some services like potable water are not fully operational for days or even months afterward."

John had recently been studying the concept of "safe enough to stay" that was employed in Christchurch, New Zealand, following the 2010-11 Canterbury earthquakes. It's a significant shift in thinking among emergency professionals from the current paradigm where locations without functioning water or sewer are deemed uninhabitable. John explained, "We've learned that keeping families together in their homes following a disaster is critical because it reduces the demand placed on emergency shelters that are traditionally operated by volunteers and non-profit organizations."

My takeaway from our conversations was any investment made into your current shelter to increase its resilience (e.g.

better insulation, more fire extinguishers) will pay dividends to you not only now, but also later during an emergency.

Mass Care Disaster Shelters

Red Cross and other "mass care" shelters offer an alternative reunification point as well as an option for you and your neighbors when you can't shelter in place (ask your local fire department about designated locations). I spoke with Dave Rasmussen, Emergency Services Manager for the American Red Cross in Seattle, about the interaction between a Prepared Neighborhood and their system of "pop-up" shelters after a widespread natural disaster.

Dave explained, "Neighborhood efforts of preparing for a wide range of disasters have proven to be essential for the most effective and speedy recoveries in this nation and around the world. One essential component to successful disaster response are well planned and well run mass care disaster shelters. Unfortunately, there will always be some homes so significantly impacted by the disaster that they are no longer a safe place to stay."

Dave went on to talk about the benefits of their shelters for folks who have not yet invested efforts into creating a Prepared Neighborhood: "Some of these residents will not have invested the energy necessary to establish the relational "links" to stay at a neighbor's home. And there are some disasters that tragically leave communities with most of its homes destroyed, leaving whole neighborhoods without shelter. Mass care shelters can be rapidly established to give these displaced people a safe refuge where their basic needs can be met, and connections to resources can be made that will accelerate one's recovery. These resources include assisting people in processing and healing from the emotional trauma experienced in the disaster."

Red Cross is always looking for additional volunteers to receive training, particularly for their winter warmth shelters that get activated annually during blizzards and winter storms. This may be a great "Step 10" duty for you to consider as your civic service. Also, consider that a Prepared Neighborhood could take in refugees from the surrounding neighborhoods to help with the crushing burden these shelters often face. Prepared citizens can create a significant base of support for our emergency professionals by hosting all but the most critically injured and distressed.

A Hub for Every Neighborhood

Different from the mass care shelters operated by the Red Cross is a new concept we're exploring on our island, one that bridges the gap between a single neighborhood and an entire town. We've nicknamed them "Hubs." In the architecture of our discussion, homes (apartments, condos, houses, etc.) are grouped together in a street, multiple streets create a neighborhood, several neighborhoods bubble up to a hub, and multiple hubs combine to create a town or section of a larger city.

Each hub is a "walkshed." Like a watershed denotes an area where from which all waters naturally flow into a single stream, river, or ocean, a "walkshed" is the location towards which citizens from one or more neighborhoods would naturally walk in search of news, medical supplies, emotional relief, food, water, and weather relief. We assume travel is via walking, bicycling, and horseback as transportation via vehicles will be difficult or impossible with roads destroyed or blocked.

For our island, each hub includes aspects of a warming shelter, medical relief tent, and communication post among other services offered. We borrowed several key design aspects from our friends down in Portland, Oregon where they call them Basic Earthquake Emergency Communications Nodes (BEECNs - pronounced "beacon"). While limited food and water supplies are available, that's not the purpose of the hub, as we're relying on the neighborhoods to provide for themselves for several weeks. The hubs will be used as distribution points for food and water supplies that arrive from outside resources, such as the National Guard, several weeks after an incident.

A primary role of the hub is as a meeting point to match those who can serve (their "Step 10" duties) with those who are in need. Immediately after an emergency, each hub is staffed by trained volunteers under the guidance of emergency professionals—whether in person or via ham radio— who have walked there after ensuring their own loved ones and neighbors are secure. The volunteer team includes both active and retired medical personnel, counselors, and civic organizers. These volunteers are given guidance from the town's emergency professionals at the Emergency Operating Center (EOC) via ham radio, with a backup communication system of "runners" which includes humans, bicycles and horses.

In addition to receiving direction from the EOC, handheld communication devices (more on that next chapter) allow each of these shelters to communicate directly with other hub shelters, Red Cross shelters, and, in time, additional mass care shelters erected by outside resources. We anticipate the hubs to be specifically communicating medical needs of incoming citizens, matching the severity of the injuries with the appropriate medical personnel scattered throughout the island.

We can make the improvements and preparations noted in this chapter to our homes, street by street and neighborhood by neighborhood, without the complexity inherent at the state or federal level. With simple agreements among a relatively small group of citizens who happen to live near each other, we can accomplish quite a bit. Despite the stereotypical bullheadedness of apartment and homeowners' associations, they are much easier to influence and change than federal and state governments!

This work can be completed piecemeal; it does not need to be part of a Great Plan rolled out by our central government. If citizens take responsibility for themselves and their neighbors, when someone in crisis cries out, "Gimme shelter!" the community will be ready to respond.

Actions: as you think about the broad definition of "shelter" for yourself and your loved ones...

☐ Go Bag – for each member of the family, including pets.

☐ Get Home Bag – for family members who travel/work away from the home.

☐ Personal heat source – a camp stove for food, Heat Sheets, sleeping bag, and proper outdoor apparel. You can find many of these items second-hand.

☐ Earthquake proof your home. Make it a group effort.

☐ Landscape for resilience. I was guilty of focusing too much on function until my wife reminded me of the importance of beauty, too.

☐ Reunification plan – start with your immediate loved ones, then bring in the neighbors, friends and extended family (who are still physically near) you'll rely on in an emergency.

☐ Take steps to retrofit your neighborhood – increase its resilience while you build strong relationships.

☐ If you've done all the above, begin planning for a Hub location for your neighborhood. Check in at bainbridgeprepares.org to see our latest efforts and the best practices we've collected.

HAM COMMUNICATIONS

EMERGENCY HUBS

NEIGHBORHOOD TRIAGE

COMMUNICATION

"A community knows itself and knows its place in a way that is impossible for a public (a nation, say, or a state). A community does not come together by a covenant, by a conscientious granting of trust. It exists by proximity, by neighborhood; it knows face to face, and it trusts as it knows."

Wendell Berry
Novelist, poet, activist, and farmer

The desire for information is a natural response after a disaster, which is made significantly more complicated when the disaster is widespread. Emergencies knock out our normal means of communication and unless we've done a bit of planning, we'll be left in the (informational) dark.

After a deafening roar, the night went silent. Nani and Bill carefully crawled out of their bed, reaching underneath to pull out their hiking shoes and leather gloves.

"Was that an earthquake?" Bill asked as they both tugged on their shoes.

Nani replied, "Either that or we just got hit by a semi-truck." They heard glass shattering in the near distance, an older windowpane slowly falling onto the hardwood floor of their kitchen. Nani flipped on her headlamp.

"Wow, what a mess," Bill said as he looked around their bedroom. They crawled over strewn furniture and a collection of chess sets dislodged from nearby shelves. The headlamps enabled them to use all four limbs while navigating the debris.

They made their way to the front door, Map Your Neighborhood guides tucked into their waistbands. Bill tore off the last page of the guide. He affixed it to the outside of their door with a piece of duct tape, showing a large "OK" to anyone passing by.

Nani went out the side door to turn off their propane tank. Although the side door's glass panes were still intact, the door itself had been ripped from its hinges and sat askew.

Nani then made her way to the kitchen and tried both her cell phone and their duplex's landline telephone. "They're both out," she told Bill. "Looks like our ability to communicate just went seriously low-tech. Let's get more clothes on and go check on the neighbors. You grab the rain jackets. I'll find the dog."

As you can tell from your reading thus far, when planning how you and your neighbors will weather a significant emergency, there are a significant number of factors and variables to consider. But at the crux of most of them is communication; timely and effective communication is the most critical component of any emergency plan.

In a widespread emergency, normal communications (e.g. telephone lines, cell towers) may not be restored for weeks or months, as we've seen in the aftermath of recent earthquakes and tsunamis. The disruption may be due to a lack of electrical power or lack of transmission capacity. Even with backup generators on cell towers, recent natural disasters have proven that the capacity of the cell towers quickly diminishes to the point at which voice calls can't get through. Our landline telephones and Internet connections may fair only slightly better as both rely heavily on electricity. And of course, no transmissions will go through if the towers and lines themselves are destroyed.

The information needed after an emergency ranges from broad (how widespread an area was affected, which dictates how soon help will arrive) to narrow (two people on our street need medical attention ASAP). By ensuring you have two-way communications for both your hyperlocal area as well as your region, you can make significantly better decisions for yourself, your family, and your neighbors.

Dr. LuAn Johnson explains:

"It is interesting to contemplate the difference between 'information' and 'communication.' Both are vital in preparing

for and responding to disasters. Information is something we give out: 'I have sprained my ankle and need help; my natural gas is leaking; I have no power and am cold; I am frightened and do not want to be alone.'

Communication is the science/art/luck of getting the information through: 'I stumbled during the ground motion of an earthquake and have severely sprained my ankle. I find my phone and discover the battery is dead. The power is out. I am beginning to feel faint. I need help.'

In Map Your Neighborhood neighborhoods, citizens know to look for a HELP sign posted in the window. My HELP card has a Band-Aid stapled to it. I use the Band-Aid as tape and hang my card in the window. In less than 10 minutes, a team of neighbors is by my side, tending to my needs.

I got to know these neighbors in a Map Your Neighborhood meeting, where we organized for such events as these. So, I know them. I trust them.

We are lucky to have a retired nurse who lives on the next block. We set up a very simple communication system with that neighborhood. Following disasters, we know to listen for the clear, high-pitched sounds of a whistle. Nothing high-tech, or even low- tech; this is non-tech so it is reliable. I have a whistle under my bed, inside my shoes. In seconds, the distress call goes out and gets through. In minutes, the nurse is handling my care.

Keys to success in this simulation are talking with my neighbors when 'times are quiet' before disasters strike, planning for all traditional communication systems to fail, and devising simple solutions to get through to those who can help.

Communication is indeed key."

Low and No-Tech Strategies

As we learned in Dr. Johnson's Map Your Neighborhood program, communications begin right away after a disaster with the placement of an OK sign or a HELP sign on your front door. Neighbors who have gathered and then sent out a team to canvas the street will use these signs to focus quickly on those most in need. Since we cannot rely on any electronic communication such as telephones immediately after an emergency, this low-tech solution is both appropriate and efficient.

In this age of interconnectedness and always-on devices that seemingly make our lives better, do we really need to plan for low and no-tech scenarios? Are there threats to our power and electronic communications beyond natural disasters, or even localized physical attacks? According to a veteran investigative journalist Ted Koppel, "Yes." In his 2015 book titled *Lights Out*, Koppel researches the possibility of a major cyber attack on our country's power grid. He finds it is not only possible but likely, and that the federal government is not prepared for it. At the time of his book publication, the US had no official plan for recovery of an attack on the national power grid. It's a worthwhile read so long as you can do a judo move on the fear, flipping it on its head to inspire positive actions rather than fear-based reactions.

The Senate Energy and Natural Resources Committee heard testimony in 2017 on EMPs and policy options for protecting energy infrastructure and improving capabilities for restoring the system after an attack. EMPs (electromagnetic pulses, blasts of electromagnetic energy from a nuclear weapon) can disrupt or destroy microprocessors and other electronic devices, a very real threat due to the spread of nuclear weapons to nations such as North Korea and the ubiquity of electronics.

Whether the power grid is taken out due to a solar storm or an EMP, the predictions on how long it will take us to recover range from a few months to a decade or longer. Large transformers will have been destroyed; over 300 could be damaged permanently in an EMP or solar storm, according to the Federal Energy Regulatory Commission. It would take several years to replace these transformers, at a significant cost running into the trillions.

From an *EMP Danger Report* submitted to Congress in 2017: "[...non-experts] ignore system upset as a vulnerability. Digital electronics can be upset by extraneous pulses of a few volts. For unmanned control systems present within the electric power grids, long-haul communication repeater stations, and gas pipelines, an electronic upset is tantamount to permanent damage. Temporary upset of electronics can also have catastrophic consequences for military operations. No electronics should be considered invulnerable to EMP unless hardened and tested to certify survivability."

Additionally, in October 2017, Congress was warned that North Korea is capable of attacking the U.S. today with a nuclear EMP bomb that could indefinitely shut down the electric power grid and kill 90 percent of all Americans within a year.

At a House hearing, experts said that North Korea could easily employ the "doomsday scenario" to decimate portions of the United States. Peter Vincent Pry, Chief of Staff with the Congressional EMP Commission, said during the hearing: "Look at what's happening in Puerto Rico now if you want to know what the consequences of an EMP attack would be."

Yikes. Scary stuff that you may want to encourage your own elected officials to act on. And in the meantime, you can protect your own electronics from an EMP by creating a simple Faraday cage with a few rolls of heavy-duty aluminum foil, some cardboard boxes and a galvanized steel trash can. You'll find plenty of DIY plans on the internet.

Methods of Communication

On a street-by-street basis, citizens can equip and train themselves in using affordable communication devices to facilitate communication. That communication will include local transmissions with folks on the other side of town, your local emergency communications center (ECC) likely run by your City Hall or fire department, and more distant transmissions with the all-important "out of area" contacts every family should have.

You can also use high-tech solutions during post-disaster Map Your Neighborhood safety sweeps. For each of these options, keep them pre-charged or stored with fresh batteries removed but attached. There is nothing worse than having a great communication device in your hand but no way to provide it power.

For both short- and long-range radios, keep in mind that the manufacturers usually overstate the distance of effectiveness. Any obstruction to the signal (trees, walls, vehicles) will cause interference and lower the effective range. Let's look at three categories of devices:

NOAA emergency weather radios: The NOAA Weather Radio All Hazards (NWR) is a nationwide network of radio stations broadcasting continuous weather information directly from the nearest National Weather Service office. NWR broadcasts official Weather Service warnings, watches, forecasts and other hazard information 24 hours a day, 7 days a week. They can be also be purchased at local hardware and camping gear stores.

Two-way radios: Short-range two-way radios (also known as walkie-talkies) offer fast and easy communication, but only when they work. These short-range devices might be useful in denser housing like apartment complexes where shouting for help to Map Your Neighborhood teammates will be ineffective. These units are easy to use and inexpensive, usually available in blister packs at your local big box retailer or (better yet) locally owned camping supply store. But keep reading for more powerful communications options.

Shortwave radios: Shortwave communication technologies like Family Radio Service (FRS) and GMRS (General Mobile Radio Service) are both readily available and affordable. These are non-cellular based communication devices, which means in the aftermath of an emergency, when cellular towers are overloaded with traffic or have been damaged, FRS and GMRS will allow you to communicate with neighbors up to a one-mile radius depending on tree/building coverage. These are excellent units to have among neighbors to use in conjunction with your Map Your Neighborhood program.

The next step up in devices is a category that includes the higher bands of GMRS and may require paying for an annual license: Marine VHF, Marine SSB, and Ham Radios.

Marine radio: With greater power and longer reach, these handheld radios are a favorite among first responders and volunteer groups like CERT. Since I live on an island, I have the Icom BC-166 marine two-way radio and recommend it for any water/boating environment. These radios are a useful addition to any Go Bag or Get Home bag if your commute involves larger bodies of water, and have value in nonemergency times when cell coverage is not reliable and you really need to reach that buddy of yours who owns a boat on a sunny summer day! They can transmit over distances from 5 to 20 miles.

Ham radio: Thankfully, we have an active radio club that can connect the various parts of our small town together even when our phone and cell systems have become overwhelmed and failed. The Bainbridge Amateur Radio Club (BARC) regularly works with the fire department and practices with our Emergency Operating Center. In the aftermath of a disaster, the BARC will be crucial in reestablishing communications across the island and beyond.

Many towns are lucky enough to have ham radio clubs, which are usually synced with their local fire departments for emergency communications, as ours is. And if your neighborhood has a ham operator living within it, count yourself lucky! These folks will be able to communicate not only directly with the professional emergency management teams working on the incident, but also with others outside the affected region who can report back on the larger scope of the emergency. Most ham operators have already taken extra steps to ensure they can continue to communicate without electricity from the grid.

How can you find out if you have an official ham radio operator living in your neighborhood? Conduct a Map Your Neighborhood meeting, of course!

We currently have ham radio installations at several of our shelters. As part of the Hub program, we're recruiting more shelters with the goal of having at least one shelter within walking distance of every neighborhood in our town. Post-disaster, after they secure their own family and immediate neighborhoods, local ham radio operators are instructed to walk to their nearest shelter for service. The shelters are either already equipped with ham radio equipment, or the operators can bring their own portable units, so they can facilitate communications.

Related, the use of both short- and long-wave handheld radios is important for family reunification plans. And it's wise to designate an out-of-area contact person to coordinate the reunification of family members within a disaster area. But what do you do when both cell and phone systems are down and you are trying to reach your out-of-area contact person? Again, Ham radio bridges the gap between local communication and long-distance communication in the no-power scenario of a natural disaster.

Ham radios are also ideal for intra-island communications in a location like mine, which has a large number of trees in the environment. Whether you live in a heavily forested area or an urban area with a significant number of buildings, Ham is the single best solution to all your emergency communication needs.

To operate a Ham radio you need a license from the FCC. But with recent changes (like dropping the Morse code requirement), you can prepare for the inexpensive test (~ $15) in just a few days using free online resources. Combined with the advent of affordable and easy (well, sort of easy) to use Ham radios, it has become much more practical to incorporate amateur radio as part of your emergency preparedness.

Ham handhelds are tiny and inexpensive. I have several, including the super popular Baofeng UV-5R. All of our island's communications with the Hubs, our ECC (Emergency

Communications Center), and our first responder teams are via Ham. These radios must be programmed before you can use them, which can be challenging even after you've passed your Ham license test. Thankfully your local Ham radio club will have one or more knowledgeable members who would be happy to do the initial programming of your radio for you.

Our final category of communication options includes satellite phones and text devices. Expensive, yes. But prices are rapidly dropping and the technology is rapidly improving.

Satellite phones: GlobalStar, Iridium, and Inmarsat phones all behave like normal cell phones for voice conversations. But they are significantly more expensive than other options and usually require the purchase of both the phone itself and a monthly access card.

The BlueCosmo brand of satellite phones was recommended to me by an acquaintance who is a UN-sanctioned emergency responder (served in the Indonesian tsunami recovery efforts and elsewhere)—particularly their GlobalStar, Iridium, and Inmarsat phones.

Satellite devices: There are also text-only devices that are still expensive, but much less so, and allow you to suspend the monthly charge when not in use.

The InReach Explorer+ is another—potentially better—option that is slightly more for the initial unit but provided by the same company that provides the satellite connection, so less finger-pointing in the user reviews when things go wrong. You can find this device at the Garmin website. Frankly, in an emergency text-only would suffice. But the added cost of the voice may be worth it for longer conversations or just ease of use.

Be aware that the text messages are handled differently than what we're used to on our cell phones. The satellite systems basically post a text message to a public or semi-public website where your loved ones can see it. Same thing for loved ones to reply: they post it on a semi-public website and the satellite-connected device quickly picks up the message.

Share When You Can: Having at least one long-range radio in each neighborhood is important for communication with other neighborhoods and the emergency professionals in the area who are gathering information and coordinating relief efforts via hubs and mass care shelters. Some disasters we can see coming—like a hurricane or a flood—and we can take appropriate measures. But many disasters, such as tornados or earthquakes, don't announce themselves in advance.

It's for those unknowable emergencies that communication before the event is so important. A small bit of discussion and planning ahead of time can effectively prepare a neighborhood to deal much more effectively with most emergencies. Part of that planning includes equipping your street with the correct communications gear since your local Ace Hardware will sell out of the low powered FMS and GMRS units within the first 30 minutes of an emergency, and may not have the higher-powered communication devices at all.

Recharging Options

When looking at emergency weather radios and two-way communication devices (both short-range and long-range), remember to plan for powering those devices in an extended emergency. And even if your smartphones are not able to connect to cellular towers or the internet, the apps they contain may still prove useful. The saying "There's an app for that" holds true for preparedness as well, with a wide variety of iOS and Android applications available, useful even in offline mode. The Red Cross family of apps are particularly well designed and worth pulling down onto your device. They have specific apps for everything from first aid to pets to specific natural disasters such as tornados and floods.

It's a great idea to keep a stock of fresh backup batteries for communication devices, but keep in mind that some devices don't accept replacement batteries (I'm looking at you, iPhone). Recharging solutions that can be shared among neighbors are also useful group purchases. In the aftermath of Hurricane Sandy, we saw a myriad of solar panel-based solutions deployed on street corners by citizens and private organizations for recharging communication devices. As we discussed in our chapter on energy, one set of chargers can power an entire street full of devices.

A few years ago, I came across one of the first rocket stove designs that lets you not only quickly heat water for cooking using small amounts of pencil-sized wood twigs, but also recharge smart devices via a USB cable. Through a clever application of thermoelectric principles, companies like Biolite allow you to heat up your soup and read a book by LED light at the same time. My non-engineering brain does not understand how the heat converts into electricity, but it works, so I'm happy!

Neighborhood Bulletin Boards

Many municipalities have designated displays around town where they will physically post news updates during an emergency, which is a system that citizens can mimic in their own neighborhoods.

Years ago our town had a bulletin board system in place for distributing information in situations in which the landline telephone systems were inoperable (this was pre-Internet and cell phones were not widely used yet). Acrylic sign holders were mounted outside Ace Hardware and similar popular locations to protect a paper insert distributed by our fire department. The system fell by the wayside for over a decade, but was recently resurrected as part of the larger hub project. Just as the advent of Little Free Libraries changes citizen behavior and traffic patterns, our town plans to use these information posts during non-emergencies to help cement their presence in the minds of citizens.

Communications Relays

A neighborhood communications relay that involves sending teenage track team members, bicycles, or horses to the town center or nearest fire station for news is another viable communication method during recovery after a large disaster.

Go! Bainbridge is a local organization we have dedicated to expanding non-vehicular travel and transportation options around our town, and is a resource for anyone walking, biking, or horse riding. It's a great example of a civic organization that makes life in your community better now, before a natural disaster, while also having a positive impact on preparedness efforts to facilitate transportation and communication after a disaster.

Emergency Operating Centers

On Bainbridge Island, the fire department is responsible for training city employees in emergency preparedness, creating an Emergency Operating Center system, and encouraging Map Your Neighborhood preparation among citizens. I asked Assistant Fire Chief, Luke Carpenter, about our emergency procedures.

He explained, "The Emergency Operating Center (EOC) system exists to provide continuity of service for the governance of our island. It is a locus for information after a large disaster, for both its collection and dissemination. In an emergency, all communities need public works to come into our EOC. If our local resources can handle it, the resources get dispatched. If we can't handle the request locally, we push it up to the county's EOC, and the process repeats there with them pulling from their county resources. From there, the request can quickly go up to state and federal levels for fulfillment."

Luke gave an example specific to Bainbridge Island and our system of neighborhood shelters: "Let's take fuel trucks as an example. If we lose power, the warming center at the Senior Center is activated. But if we lose power for an extended period, their propane-fired system will need to be refilled as it only has a six-day supply of fuel. That pending need comes to us, and our EOC looks at our facilities. Because there is no propane storage on the island, we would pass that request on to the next communication node off our island: the Kitsap County Department of Emergency Management (KCDEM) EOC. The propane would likely be delivered via barge if the bridge is down and the ferries are not operating."

I spoke with Susan May, who was the KCDEM Program Coordinator for years and frequented our island to conduct CERT training. I asked her about the county's role with individual towns during both emergency and normal times. Susan explained, "During a disaster, the KCDEM provides assistance when local resources become exhausted. Our main concern—as is with every first responder—is to protect and keep safe the citizens of Kitsap County to the best of our ability. We work behind the scenes to ensure every agency responsible for public safety, health, and welfare receives the tools and manpower to provide the most suitable and adequate service during times of need. This would include broad-brush information sharing to our community providing protective recommendations, situational updates, and informational forecasts on when we can return to day-to-day operations and normal living."

We talked further about the shared communication goals of emergency preparedness professionals regardless of level—from the city all the way up to federal—with citizens out in the neighborhoods during good times or bad. Susan commented, "Our goal is to be the communication tool that provides the information; that local perspective which may not come from big media outlets. During non-emergency times, we provide advice so citizens can learn how to take care of themselves during disasters and how to prepare their personal surroundings to limit their exposure to harm."

Backup Systems

To further facilitate communications, my citizen-led team contracted with the San Francisco-based software development team *Recovers* to create the backup systems that our town would be able to use—with or without power—for communications among neighborhoods, our shelters, and our emergency professionals. Bainbridge Island was the first *Recovers* project to be worked on proactively, before a natural disaster struck. Most of their clients are in the middle of experiencing a flood or the aftermath of a tornado.

The *Recovers* team was responsive to our numerous requests for tweaking their online tools to better fit a team working on preparedness rather than a team responding to an existing emergency. Their CEO and Co-Founder, Caitria O'Neill, spoke with me weekly as we built the Bainbridge Island site on their platform. I asked Caitria specifically about the importance of communications from her unique high-tech startup perspective. She's spoken of it often, even recording a popular TED Talk with her sister and Co-Founder.

Caitria told me, "Both disaster preparedness and recovery depend upon the ability of a community to communicate with itself and the outside world. Every community has a wide range of technical capability. There will be extremely tech-savvy households standing right next to a resident who chooses not to have any devices that connect to the Internet. When trying to reach people with information on how to prepare and recovery information in the case of a disaster, you have to keep this in mind. A working system has to continue functioning when the web goes down in an emergency."

Caitria and her team had already worked at dozens of natural disaster scenes before we met. During a trip to our island to test new features of the software, they stayed at our home, which led to interesting conversations around the kitchen table. Here's Caitria again, "In the aftermath of Hurricane Sandy, we saw a few amazing communication systems spring up. New York City residents with web connectivity and tech expertise scraped the Internet for information, updates, and explanations of how to access aid. They then shared this information using a variety of social media tools and other software. People who saw it could print off a resource sheet and distribute it in one of the 'dead zones' to those who could not access and collect this information themselves. Gaps in Internet access were covered by volunteers who knew that they could help by walking around with information on foot."

We talked further about the wide range of possible tools citizens could use for effective and efficient communication, from high-tech to low-tech to no-tech. Despite her young age, Caitria's wisdom and field experience shined as she commented, "Really, the tools don't matter as much as the plan. You can train residents right now where to find information to print and distribute after a disaster. You can leverage a door-to-door volunteer who is using an iPad or paper forms for data collection. The important thing is to start planning and to assume different levels of tech capability for each neighborhood."

It is important to note that recovery estimates are usually measured in months to years, not days to weeks. Using my northwest neighbor as just one example, the Oregon Seismic Safety Policy Advisory Commission published the following recovery/rebuild estimates after a significant earthquake (highway I-5 is the primary north-south transportation avenue connecting Vancouver, BC to Portland, OR and beyond):

Service	I-5 Corridor	Coast
Electricity	1-3 months	3-6 months
Drinking water/sewer	1 month-1 year	1-3 years
Schools	18 months	18 months
Police and fire	2-4 months	3 years
Healthcare facilities	18 months	3 years
Major highways	6-12 months	1-3 years
Telecommunications	6-12 months	6-12 months

Local Media

In addition to leveraging communications experts from afar, we've also turned to experts in our own backyard to help our emergency preparedness professionals quickly and efficiently get out the word during and after emergencies.

The local go-to source for daily news on our island for several years was a website called Inside Bainbridge, published by Julie Hall and Sarah Lane (Sarah edited early versions of blog posts which eventually became chapters in this book). Just as other local citizens have their own "Step 10" in the Map Your Neighborhood procedures, Sarah and Julie volunteered their digital communication skills to help our EOC and local ham radio operators with navigating social media and texting for the dissemination of emergency response information.

In the last couple of years, social media has radically changed public perception of both manmade conflicts (e.g. the Arab Spring) and natural disasters. Citizen expectations for sites like Facebook, Twitter, and Instagram have morphed from viewing them as a source for one-way information consumption to a tool for two-way information transfer. These channels are being monitored by emergency professionals for real-time, location-specific data so they can make better decisions.

I asked Sarah about her preparation for post-disaster communication:

With our increased awareness of what happens to the media in an emergency, in some ways it feels like we are returning to an older time, a time with a town crier or a posted broadside. But really what's happening is we are learning to be more agile and to use the wide array of tools available to us. We start with our website. When that goes down, we use our phones and post via Twitter. When the cell towers are down, we turn to ham radio and send out news that way. I feel we're very fortunate to have a forward-thinking Fire Department at the helm, inviting us to participate in the process early on, well before the emergency, because they have a good understanding of the options and the way the different technologies work and then stop working. They understand that commanding an audience and knowing how to deliver the news are essential, no matter what the medium.

Starting the Conversation Before the Disaster

Beginning the conversation with that audience before a wide-scale emergency occurs is crucial. Citizens can alleviate much of the pressure put on our preparedness professionals in a time of widespread crisis by coordinating efforts directly among neighborhoods to leverage our huge range of collective skills.

As we discussed earlier, one Map Your Neighborhood street may have three medically trained citizens living on it, and another may have two structural engineers. When a disaster strikes, after each Map Your Neighborhood street has ensured its initial stability, residents can begin to communicate with other nearby streets to assess their needs. Being able to swap a nurse for a structural engineer greatly benefits both locations.

Communication is one of the building blocks of good relationships, whether it is with your loved ones or the rest of your neighborhood. The success of your Map Your Neighborhood project relies on open dialogue with the rest of your neighbors at least once a year. During those sessions you can update one another on any new special needs, changes in the home, and additional skills you've learned that year that can be of benefit to the neighborhood.

Meeting the Neighbors: We do our Map Your Neighborhood annual get-together as a post-holiday party each year, part of the "we can survive another winter together" set of winter holiday parties that happen in the dreary Pacific Northwest, usually set in January after the business of the season has begun to wane a bit. We spend about 45 minutes discussing Map Your Neighborhood and the rest of the evening socializing. That's how we handle updates for a single street.

Bainbridge Islander Leslie Marshall has spent several years combining individual streets in her Commodore neighborhood to form a cohesive Map Your Neighborhood group spanning 65+ single-family homes. When moving beyond a single street with MYN materials, you'll quickly find need of secondary systems for the organization beyond just an MYN flipchart that might include email lists, a spreadsheet, social media group connections, and a bit of shoe leather.

Leslie gave me this insight for coordinating that many neighbors, saying: "People have busy enough schedules that it is difficult to find a time that works for even a majority of the invitees, let alone everyone. What has worked for me is to go to every home in our neighborhood, explain to the adult who answers the door just what the MYN initiative is all about, and have that person fill out a questionnaire right then."

But what to do when no one is at home when you stop by? Persistence is key for the citizen activist (which is likely you, if you're reading this). Leslie explained, "If no one is home when I visit or if it is just not a good time for a conversation, then I keep returning until I can have the chat and collect the data. (Some of the conversations continued for an hour or more!) If the person declines to participate, which happened for just two homes out of 65 or more, I thank them and do not return."

In addition to getting her outside for some fresh air and exercise, Leslie found the building of trust to be a significant benefit of this face-to-face approach. She told me of examples of neighbors walking with her as they visited additional homes to facilitate introductions. Her larger neighborhood also made use of the email distribution list when dealing with a rash of burglaries. One final encouraging word from Leslie: "This kind of approach obviously takes a lot of time, but the results are impressively thorough. And it is a great way for a newcomer (which I was when this all started) to get connected in a deep way to one's community."

Conversations within our neighborhoods about preparedness are not just relegated to what we do after some undefined future emergency. To build true resilience and create true sustainability in our community and our individual lives, we can take action now. Rather than lamenting the latest natural disaster or foolishly thinking "it can't happen here," consider taking positive, community-building action instead. Start with a discussion with just one of your neighbors about checking in on each other after a disaster. You'll see it blossom from there. And enjoy the peace of mind those new relationships bring!

Actions: do your planning now so you are not left in the (informational) dark...

☐ Revisit your MYN plan and see how communication devices could support that work with your neighbors.

☐ On your daily walk, get an idea of how far you can travel by foot to solicit information from and share news with neighbors.

☐ Research the various devices we discussed and decide on the best device/s for your family and your neighborhood.

☐ Set up and maintain neighborhood bulletin boards: digital and in the physical world.

☐ Designate neighborhood communications relay systems.

LOCOMOTION

PEDAL POWER

NON-FUEL ALTERNATIVES

TRANSPORTATION

"Every time I see an adult on a bicycle, I no longer despair for the future of the human race."

H. G. Wells
Author

Our dependence upon the automobile to conduct our daily lives will be cut short suddenly after an emergency, whether it is short or long term. But perhaps no more "happy motoring" is a good thing?

Ross and Lisa were on their way to town one Saturday afternoon to replenish their neighborhood's cache of medical supplies. Slowly.

With the bridge still under repair after the earthquake, the only fuel being transported onto the island via barge was designated for the town's emergency vehicles. Most folks—including Ross and Lisa—had run out of fuel for their personal vehicles several days ago.

Although the city's Public Works team—with plenty of help from local building contractors—had cleared downed trees and power lines from the primary roads, the lack of fuel meant walking and bicycling had become the most common mode of transportation. A new, more deliberate pace of life had resulted, with longer conversations taking place as people walked together.

"Listen," said Ross suddenly, "what's that sound?"

Startled at the sight of nine large beautiful horses in a fast trot coming around a bend in the path, Ross and Lisa quickly moved to the side of the trail.

"Hello!" cried out Barbara McChord. "We were just heading to your neighborhood with food. They called in this morning on the ham radio with a shopping list."

Indeed, all nine horses were laden with saddlebags bursting with produce from the now-daily farmer's market at the center of town. Lisa shot Barbara a wide grin, thinking of the delicious group dinner they would be able to fix this evening with their neighbors.

Locomotion

Let's begin with the big picture of transportation in North America and then work our way down to our neighborhoods. While we are seeing promising developments in electric-powered test flights, it's not clear how long we'll be able to continue national and international travel via planes. The current configuration of the airline industry is doomed with their massive carbon hit, significant fossil fuel requirements, and the generally unprofitable nature. Trains offer an ability to travel nationwide, albeit at a slower pace than air travel, and enjoy a more hopeful future because of private investments made by the likes of Warren Buffet and Bill Gates.

In terms of oil use, transportation is the largest and fastest-growing energy sector in recent decades, mostly from new demand for personal-use vehicles. Our dependence on automobiles for personal transportation and on the trucking industry for moving goods stands in the way of making long distance travel more sustainable. I'm a big fan of zero-emission electric vehicles (assuming they can be recharged with renewable energy), but with our dwindling resources, electric vehicles may be too little too late.

What are the alternatives available for the daily short-haul transportation of people and goods in the event that regional roadways are interrupted by a widespread emergency or a long-term emergency like the gas shortages of the 1970's? If an emergency scenario arises in which our inflow of oil is severely curtailed, we must be able to function with little to no oil-assisted transportation for an extended period of time. Whether it is for conducting daily errands around town or making a once-a-decade hurricane or wildfire evacuation trip with your Go Bags, creating multiple options for transportation makes sense for both lessening our impact on the earth and building resilience into our lives.

Islands Everywhere

In an emergency, we can assume that it will not be just our fuel sources that are severely limited. Physical access to clear roads and pathways will also be blocked by destroyed buildings, water, downed trees and broken power lines. In a very real sense, the hyperlocal area you are in can become just like an island, with easy access cut off in every direction.

For emergencies that are preceded by ample advance warning such as hurricanes, the wisest use of fuel may be to vacate the area. But for sudden emergencies like earthquakes, it may be wiser to conserve transportation fuel, shelter in place, using your remaining fuel to help those around you by transporting them to nearby shelters for medical attention or weather relief. Many citizens waste precious fuel driving around right before and after a disaster looking for emergency supplies like bottled water. A small bit of planning and self-discipline will help you conserve that precious fuel resource for more acute needs, like medical emergencies.

Living on an actual island with the very real possibility of being cut off by a collapsed bridge and a nonfunctioning ferry system makes me take to heart any wisdom offered by my elders. Years ago, someone encouraged me to always refill my fuel tanks when they hit the one-half mark. This bit of wisdom is just as relevant to people on the mainland. Many smaller towns can be cut off from supply lines with the closure of one or two highways, which would stop the inflow of food, fuel, and other needed materials. And while major cities have multiple thoroughfares connecting them to the surrounding countryside, the sheer number of people in residence means supplies would be immediately depleted.

People Power

For transporting ourselves and smaller amounts of goods, we can rely on human and animal power. But how many of our citizens can walk multiple miles, day after day?

I spoke with our local Striders Club— a local group of very fit retirees—about personal responsibility as part of their emergency preparedness plans for natural disasters. One of their vocal members told me: "It will take the world-class local, state, and federal emergency response apparatus we have in the United States several days—if not weeks—to come to our aid. This is not an indictment of their desire or ability to help. Instead, it is the stark reality of confronting a catastrophic situation where the needs of those impacted greatly exceed the capacity of those dedicated to providing help."

We talked further about the importance of maintaining personal health. They felt it was critical for them to do everything they can to be prepared to take care of themselves for at least a week. (I gave them a gentle reminder that FEMA now says 14 days and that they live on an island, which means they should consider an additional 7-14 days.)

Since the purpose of their club is to stay physically fit while exploring the area's walking trails, it was no surprise that they also noted an oft-overlooked consideration: the importance of taking care of yourself so that you are physically fit and better able to cope with the manual labor associated with responding to the devastation that will surround you. We discussed what they felt they were likely to confront: a damaged home with its contents strewn about, floors covered with broken glass, blocked and/or damaged roads preventing the use of cars, and more. To move around in that kind of situation, you will have to be able to lift and carry loads, walk long distances, and perhaps ride a bicycle to obtain supplies and other assistance.

Speaking of bicycles, in addition to finding immediate benefits of maintaining our personal health in non-emergency times, we'll find similar benefits in the maintenance of our non-motorized gear such as bicycles. I spoke with Jeff Groman, the founder of Classic Cycle here on the island and an avid bicyclist enthusiast, about the importance of maintaining bicycling: "One of the things I discovered early in my career was the importance of having a bicycle ready to go at all times. The bicycle is one of the most important inventions of the 19th century and one of the top 10 inventions that changed the world. When getting from A to B you can always depend on the reliability of the bicycle. It is by far the most efficient means of transportation for almost everything. One only has to look at the Netherlands to see the possibilities."

If the power goes out and there's no ready supply of gasoline, the bicycle will be the most useful tool in your garage or storage unit. When you need to get somewhere as quickly as possible, such as the closest mass care shelter, the efficient power transfer a bicycle allows is unbeatable. Jeff commented on the technology behind this amazing but often overlooked resource, "The intermediate level of technology is quite simple compared to a motorized vehicle. With a little bit of technical skill, a bicycle is easily maintained and will provide reliable transportation in all situations. We have a plethora of machines ready at all times at our home for recreation, transportation, and emergencies. On an island like Bainbridge, it's possible to get from every part of the island to the main town in less than 30 minutes."

Critical Supply Network

Our island actually sits in the middle of the Puget Sound, so we've created our own emergency flotilla of private citizens, which can be activated by our EOC to transport critical supplies and essential staff on and off the island, assist with coastline surveys of damage, and assist with oil spill responses. The flotilla is managed by our Harbormaster, who recruited volunteers and their private vessels to assist when activated as their "Step 10." After working through the first nine steps of their Map Your Neighborhood program, their civic duty kicks in and they report with their vessel to the Harbormaster for deployment.

Whether you are ferrying your supplies across a large bay or a small but fast-flowing river after a bridge has collapsed, you'll need an overland network to get those critical supplies to your population centers.

Nonfuel Strategies: A forced, if temporary, switch in our infrastructure system via a natural disaster will bring new (actually old) technologies to light. When we no longer enjoy clear paved roads and have no further access to fossil fuels, how will we view transportation of goods and people in a bioregion? Navigable rivers and calm waterways are an option. But it is most likely that bicycles will return to their place of glory as the marvels of engineering that they are.

Jason F. McLennan's industry-leading standard, the Living Building Challenge framework, fully integrates the concept of transportation through his lens of architecture. Jason often talks of the "living transportation" paradigm: By making human- and renewably-powered methods of transportation a societal norm, we can do a judo move and flip the old fossil fuel-driven system on its head.

Jason knows what he is talking about. He's one of the world's most influential individuals in the field of architecture and the green building movement, winner of numerous awards, and author of several key books in his field. The Living Building Challenge is just one of several paradigm-busting entities he's created over the years. He's a fellow rebel rouser and a good friend here on Bainbridge Island.

One day, Jason and I discussed bicycle-based alternative vehicles such as the ELF, a pedal-powered solar hybrid "car." He owns one of the first ELFs in production. Jason observed, "Imagine if we used vehicles like this for the majority of our in-town commuting. We'd be healthier and safer, have more fun commuting, and our cities could begin to be reshaped around a more human scale."

When an emergency includes no- or low-power scenarios, walking, bicycling, and horseback riding will all find their uses. Towns that have active riding clubs for both bicycles and horses have an excellent resource for transportation that does not rely directly on fuel. In a longer emergency, assuming their feed can be provided, horses can also be used to assist in the moving of heavy machinery to clear rubble and roads.

Betsey Wittick of Laughing Crow Farm talked horses with me at a recent farmer's market: "Draft horses are an example of smaller-scale technology appropriate to certain farms, particularly those going beyond organic to something like biodynamic. The online Farm Hack community that is creating new implements for horses is encouraging."

The Farm Hack community is a worldwide community of farmers that build and modify their own tools, sharing the designs both online and in person. Take a peek at their work at farmhack.org; it's a fascinating mixture of high-tech robotics, low-tech ingenuity, and a deep connection to land and animals.

She added: "Draft work requires a different approach to farming than using a tractor, primarily because you are depending on a living being to provide the 'horsepower,' one with its own needs, attitudes, and opinions. For those willing to learn what it takes to farm this way, there is an added benefit: one of a spiritual connection with the horse. That's something you don't get with an internal combustion engine."

Community-Owned Heavy Machinery and Tools

The availability of heavy machinery for transport of goods and materials and for emergency work such as removing debris and fallen trees is a significant concern for emergency professionals and citizens in their neighborhoods. Marcin Jakubowski has an interesting solution: His *Global Village Construction Set*, which is sometimes called a "civilization starter kit," features a wide range of tools that could be shared among several micro-farmers and permaculture enthusiasts. The kit sells for around USD $10,000—the more folks who are sharing the tools, the more affordable the kit becomes.

But most areas already have plenty of existing heavy machinery on location. Through a series of Memorandum of Understanding (MOU) documents with developers, our town is developing access to the privately-owned heavy machinery that is already out in neighborhoods on construction sites. In the case of a wide-scale disaster, these MOUs can be activated by our City Manager (similar to a mayor) to pull in needed heavy machinery and tools to clear away rubble and make roads passable for emergency vehicles. It's worth noting that their focus will be the core infrastructure of the city as well as the access points (such as our only bridge), and not clearing away rubble in neighborhood streets.

As citizens, we'll need to be able to remove debris and rubble ourselves, which should be kept in mind when deciding where to store your emergency supplies. Consider from which location would it be easier to retrieve your gear and supplies: a standalone shed or your basement. Assuming both structures fall down during a natural disaster, it is significantly easier to dig through the thin splintered walls of a shed than thousands of pounds of rubble generated by the collapse of a home or an apartment building.

Community Pathways

Whether you are on a horse, bicycle, or your own two feet, the pathways that take you from neighborhood to neighborhood are crucial. Thankfully, many cities maintain maps of non-motorized trails; ours even includes kayak trails for nearby shores and camping locations. The map serves as a good visual of the positive things that happen when civic and private groups cooperate, in our case City Hall, Parks District, Open Space Commission, and the private nonprofit Bainbridge Island Land Trust. A visit to your local Chamber of Commerce or City Hall will let you know if these non-motorized maps exist. If not, it would be a fun project to take on for your area!

Let's look at another municipality's work in alternative transportation; return with me to Burlington, Vermont. Back in the 1980s, Burlington's mayor at the time—Bernie Sanders—invested in bike paths along their scenic waterfront to reduce automobile traffic and open up space that was previously inaccessible. More recently, as part of their new focus on becoming "net zero" (when an entity generates as much energy as it consumes), the current mayor, Miro Weinberger, is locating electric vehicle recharging stations at key locations and radically expanding their protected bicycle pathways. Weinberger said, "Stats show the existence of protected lanes increased usage by 300 to 500 percent because there are a whole lot of people who don't feel safe co-mingled with vehicles."

I sought out Dana Berg, the founder of *GO! Bainbridge*, to speak with me about the importance of their mission to promote these non-motorized pathways on our island: "This is a timely conversation as my nephew is here from Brooklyn and he was telling me how crazy it was during Hurricane Sandy and how everyone was surprised at how tenuous things are, especially when there are no shipments of gasoline. We often forget that our society runs on oil. Most people and most goods are transported by cars and trucks fueled by oil. During emergencies, that system can be disrupted very quickly. The power may be out to pump the fuel or there may be no way for fuel to get to the fueling stations. Luckily, we have alternative transportation right at our feet."

We spoke about the many benefits to a community when transportation of goods and people happens via something other than a car, whether it is during good times or bad. Dana observed, "Walking and biking are historic ways of getting to places and are still available to most people today. An average walker travels at 3 miles per hour, a cyclist at 12 miles per hour. And during a disaster, when roads may be impassable, walkers and cyclists can often find trails and detours that get them past these hazards and blockages. And the only fuel needed is some food. Keeping a bike in good working order is an important part of your emergency preparedness plan. And taking some trips in your neighborhood by foot or bike on a regular basis will help you keep in touch with neighbors. It is easy to stop and chat when moving about without a car and a great way to stay connected with your local area."

Of course, Bainbridge Island is not alone in creating transportation corridors that do not rely on automobiles. Active bicycling communities usually thrive in the same areas where sustainability or preparedness initiatives do. Witness Bellingham's popular bike paths in Washington State where there is a local *Transition Town* movement for Whatcom County. It's also the home to the *Sustainable Connections* organization; both of which have a serious interest in moving transportation beyond oil.

And consider Shelby County in Tennessee, which reversed its listing as one of the "worst cities" by *Bicycling Magazine* in 2008, when it had fewer than two miles of bicycle paths, to now include over 160 miles of pathways. Their local preparedness group, *Ready Shelby*, is benefiting from this commitment to sustainability and community-building.

The financial commitment to creating and maintaining these non-motorized pathways also proves to be a good investment. As Bobby Allyn from *The New York Times* reported,

The mayor's office says that the potential economic ripple effect of bike lanes is proof that they are a sound investment.

A study in 2011 by the University of Massachusetts found that building bike lanes created more jobs—about 11 per $1 million spent—than any other type of road project. Several bike shops here have expanded to accommodate new cyclists, including Midtown Bike Company, which recently moved to a location three times the size of its former one. "The new lanes have been great for business," said the manager, Daniel Duckworth.

Wanda Rushing, a professor at the University of Memphis and an expert on urban change in the South, said bike improvements were of a piece with a development model sweeping the region: bolstering transportation infrastructure and population density in the inner city.

"Memphis is not alone in acknowledging that sprawl is not sustainable," Dr. Rushing said. "Economic necessity is a pretty good melding substance."

Bicycling is also a pathway to riches, as the online persona, Mr. Money Mustache, explains. An expert at living well below your means (and thus enjoying life to a much more significant degree), Mr. MM writes regularly (www.mrmoneymustache.com) about the financial benefits of bicycling layered on top of the health and preparedness reasons to have bikes around:

The fundamental reason for the Bike's status as the Greatest Invention of All Time is its unique combination of simplicity, efficiency, and incredibly good health benefits. Interestingly enough, those are the opposite of a car's attributes. The Bike is simple with just a few moving parts, simple enough for most people to maintain entirely on their own without paying a mechanic.

But another side effect is that bikes are good for your wealth. Let's start with the bare minimum: any mileage you put on your bike instead of your car saves you about 50 cents per mile in gas, depreciation, and wear and maintenance. From these savings alone, doing a couple of bike errands per day (4 miles) in place of car errands will add up to $10,752 over ten years.

But the benefits are greater than that, of course. Once you get into bicycling, it may grow on you. You may be able to go without a car, or you might find, like me, that having an expensive car is no longer useful as a status symbol to you.

This would allow you to keep a less expensive car (saving another $30,000+ over ten years). You might find that biking around becomes a source of leisure as well as transportation. This would displace other more expensive leisure *activities. Driving to the stadium to watch a monster truck rally with the family ($100) could be replaced by biking along the creek path and wading around in the waterfalls ($0). Replacing even $10 per week of paid leisure with free biking would net you another $7680.*

Then there are incalculable things like health and productivity. But we are bold enough to calculate them here. By riding to work instead of driving, you are boosting your mood and your mental focus. This allows you to work smarter and longer. It also makes you look better. These factors will allow you to earn at least an average of 5% more than your unfit counterparts would after various raises and job switches kick in.

For a worker at the $50,000 annual level, this is a $2500/year boost ($37,500 after ten years). Then there are the reduction of doctor visits and prescription drugs, which will benefit you as you get older. This is a large future sum, but let's estimate the net present value to be about $500/year ($7500 over ten). And we haven't even gotten into the effect of greater health on your overall enjoyment of life.

Rethinking Our Urban Areas

Remaking our neighborhoods and towns around pedestrians is a long-term project, but definitely worthwhile to make our living and working areas more sustainable and able to withstand shocks like natural disasters. As author and architectural critic James Howard Kunstler often argues, the end of cheap energy (read: oil) will force us to return to smaller-scale, agrarian-focused communities.

I spoke with Jonathan Davis about this. He is a green architect, the principal of Davis Studio Architecture + Design, and a proponent of One Planet design principles. He said, "In our current project, we are creating a community that will be zero carbon by 2020. Partially this is through homes that are extremely energy efficient with on-site photovoltaics. These net-zero homes have photovoltaic solar panel arrays that will generate enough energy to offset that used by each house, thereby greatly reducing monthly energy costs and, more importantly, their carbon footprint. The homes are warm and welcoming, using interior finishes that have been selected for both their sustainable qualities and also to create inviting and comfortable living spaces."

As a forward-thinking architect, Jonathan is concerned with more than just the building envelope itself. His sustainable thinking extends to the areas around his buildings, as well as the access points to them via various transportation methods. Jonathan observed, "A significant aspect of our zero net energy community is related to transportation. Due to the project's location in an urban core, we take advantage of nearby, local facilities for residents like grocery stores, pharmacies, cafes, and schools that are within easy walking and biking distance. While we've added a zero-emission automobile for use by our homeowners, much of the transportation needs of the community are created by people power."

As we look into the future of transportation in both normal and emergency times, it looks like we'll be "back to the future" with an enjoyable focus on transportation methods from before the advent of the automobile. We're already seeing sail craft—both large and small—being used for the transportation of goods in protected waterways like the Puget Sound and on navigable rivers. A significant increase in citizens bicycling and walking will make our towns healthier and more resilient!

Actions: Bicycles, bicycles, bicycles! Oh, and a good pair of walking shoes...

☐ Have alternative transportation ready: keep bicycles maintained and have a set of spare parts in storage. Local bike shops offer how-to skills seminars which are fun for folks of all ages.

☐ Keep yourself in fit condition to endure an emergency situation while helping others.

☐ Always keep automobiles prepared for emergencies with full fuel tanks; refill once they hit the 50% mark.

☐ Find like-minded neighbors to discuss an investment in community-owned machinery.

☐ Identify, establish and maintain walking, bicycle and

horse trails. Ensure paths and walkways are well maintained and clearly signposted.

EDUCATION

KITS

C. E. R. T.

GROUP RESILIENCE

"Those who run from death, like the survivalists in their bunkers and the permaculturalists in the forest, also run from life. As an EMT, as a CEMP member, as a latecomer to the world of outdoor adventure, I'd discovered that the opposite is also true: those who run to death also run to life.

When you walk to the very edge of the abyss, and you lean over and peer as deep into the blackness as you possibly can, and maybe you even lower a hand into it and pull someone out who's not supposed to be there, that's when you feel alive.

I've learned it isn't actually survival these skills bring. It's peace of mind."

Neil Strauss
Author, journalist, and ghostwriter

This chapter focuses on how trained or skilled individuals can band together for the benefit of the neighborhood. In each area that we discuss we'll see that our efforts as a group are so much greater than if we each tried to go it on our own.

As we stated at the beginning of this book, our hard-working first responders (firefighters, police, EMTs) will not be coming out to check on citizens in neighborhoods in the aftermath of a natural disaster. They will be overwhelmed repairing the area's infrastructure. This is when mutual aid among citizens comes into play.

Mutual aid is neighbors taking care of neighbors—working as a team—in the aftermath of a natural disaster so our first responders can do their jobs more effectively. Every citizen has their own unique skills to bring forward for the benefit of the neighborhood. Individual self-sufficiency is not only unattainable but also undesirable. **Group resilience is a much better goal and solution.** As groups are comprised of individuals, these individuals have a responsibility to themselves and their communities to discover their unique talents and share with others.

And if the earthquake or other widespread natural disaster does not occur in our lifetimes? Well, our lives are that much richer with our new neighborly relations and the additional skills we've learned together.

Most of the new apple trees were destroyed. And Ross was frustrated.

He knew he should have put up a deer barrier before planting the bare root trees on Friday. But he thought the new trees would be okay for a couple of nights while he was traveling for work. After a late return flight Sunday night, he awoke Monday morning to find several hundred dollars' worth of fruit trees destroyed, the bark stripped by hungry deer.

As Ross stood sullenly in his front yard, his neighbor Amy walked over from across the street, carrying a bundle of bamboo. "Got any wire?" she asked.

"Sure," replied Ross. "I have some 14-gauge wire left over from another project. What's up with the bamboo stakes?"

"Well, I shooed off the deer family from your fruit trees earlier this morning at dawn—saw them when I was making coffee—but I was too late to stop the damage. They looked like they had been camped out eating for a while. So I thought I'd teach you a cool setup to temporarily protect newly planted trees. It just takes a few minutes."

"Thanks. I owe you one. Where did you learn this bamboo wire trick?" asked Ross.

"I took a homesteading class last year with Tom who lives next door. Then we experimented on the trees in both our backyards. It works great. Let me show you," Amy replied.

Neighbors, not Government

Former FEMA Administrator, W. Craig Fugate, in his article *The Public as a Resource* from Government Technology Magazine, stated:

The public is one of our greatest resources in times of crisis and should be included as an important part of your resilience planning and training. The bigger the disaster, the less likely the government can provide the best response.

In the case of almost any disaster, the fastest response will be from your neighbor. We should put a higher priority on getting the private sector operational after a disaster. If these businesses get up and running, it takes tremendous stress off the government and government resources... we must include giving the people back a sense of control in our preparedness planning.

We need to give people the OK to help one another, and give businesses the OK — and the resources — to get back on track so they can help those people who cannot help themselves.

Breadth and Depth of Skills

No person is an island—especially in the aftermath of a large natural disaster. In decades past, we've seen a number of so-called self-sufficiency experts encouraging us to learn a wide range of skills so we can "go it alone." Especially when paired with an attitude towards hunkering down in a remote bunker, that's just plain bad advice. Being a lone ranger is dangerous. A resilient community is a much stronger response to any emergency or disaster, short or long term.

To go it alone, the list of personal skills you would need to gather in your personal toolbox is daunting, even if you are seeking mere proficiency and not deep expertise. Self-sufficiency is not realistically attainable for the vast majority of citizens, nor is it particularly desirable. Group resilience—being able to rely on your local friends and trusted neighbors—is a much better approach to both emergency preparedness and living sustainably.

As we seek to become better community members, it's our responsibility to improve our individual skill sets. Not seeking to become an expert in everything, but following our natural passions and interests. What do you already know that you can share with others? Perhaps you have mastered food preservation methods like canning or smoking, or perhaps you have sage financial advice about eliminating debt and living below one's means. Everyone has something they can learn. We also each have something we can teach.

When the emergency occurs, we'll have need of every skill set, even ones not often used. At any given time, every neighborhood in the country likely has at least one pregnant resident. While the act of giving birth might be an occurrence just once or twice in a woman's life, should that need to occur in the weeks after a natural disaster when her normal medical care is not available, midwifery skills will be in sudden high demand in her neighborhood. Learning and practicing new skills—like splitting wood or installing drip irrigation in your vegetable garden—by yourself is good, but doing so with friends and neighbors is better. And making new relationships within your community during these classes is the best! Many towns and neighborhoods offer ample free opportunities to build new relationships and personal skills at the same time. On our island, we can take classes related to preparedness, homesteading, and building resilience from a number of organizations.

We can learn about growing food at local garden supply stores, participate in CPR classes offered by our Fire Department, learn bicycle maintenance from one of our local bike shops, and learn about building personal health and wellness via any number of our local gyms, yoga studios, and counselors. We can even learn to forage our forests and shorelines through our City Hall's Parks & Recreation Department. There is something for everyone!

My wife Susan and I recently launched a nonprofit collaboration to organize all these teachers spread across so many different organizations. The collaboration brings focus and attention to these homesteading and preparedness topics. We've even managed to attract a number of new teachers who were not previously offering classes at all. It's a joy to see citizens teaching others citizens, increasing the resilience in our area one cohort at a time.

Although we live in a beautiful area of North America, it does come with some inherent dangers (we're looking at you, Seattle Faultline!). Thankfully, we can build physical and emotional resilience into our lives now by learning the needed skills in preparedness and practical living that will be helpful later, in a time of need. The homesteading and preparedness classes support our community's journey to become the most prepared town in Washington State by empowering North Kitsap County citizens to acquire practical skills that build resilience. You can do the same in your area!

We've created a series of year-round classes which (conveniently!) correspond to the chapters in this book: growing and preserving food (including trapping/hunting, more on that in the next chapter with firearm safety), basic plumbing and electrical repair, outdoor survival including making fires and shelter (including sewing/mending of your gear), amateur radio, bicycle maintenance, and medical/disaster training (e.g. CPR, first aid, CERT).

It's up to you and the specific needs of your family and neighborhood to decide the priority order in which to pursue this new knowledge. I'd encourage you to reach out to local family, friends, and neighbors to take the classes together as that significantly contributes to your retention and enjoyment of learning new skills.

As one example, Els Heyne is the Marketing & Sustainability Director at my local garden supply store, Bay Hay & Feed. She is intimately familiar with the joys and perils of growing your own food. We spoke about learning food-growing skills from previous generations via community classes: "Not that long ago 90 percent of the people grew their own food, but now only five percent grow the food for the rest of us. Many people lost the basic skills and knowledge to grow their own food, so we're teaching people some of those skills again. From how to raise your own chickens to how to keep bees, we are adding more and more classes for these important skills."

Many of the skills that we need to collectively relearn are related to food production and preservation, staying comfortable without electricity no matter the season, and other topics that generally fall into a category we call "homesteading." Some communities will still have elders from whom they can directly learn. Others will need to learn via books, blogs, and apps. As we discussed in the Communications chapter, the Red Cross series of apps is particularly broad. In addition, apps like WildEdible and SunSurvey are a bit like having a college professor hiking with you through the forest or planning out the best location for your neighborhood vegetable garden.

The list of skills that we could seek out can be overwhelming—from woodworking and blacksmithing to foraging and camping—if we allow it to be. But if we each follow our natural passions and seek out new knowledge in the areas that interest us first, we can be assured that, as a group, we'll have covered most of our bases.

Medical Training

Regarding medical training, first aid kits are only as useful as the user's knowledge allows. Everyone you know—including children—should pursue FEMA's "Until Help Arrives" program (available online and in person), basic first aid, and basic CPR training. For older teens and adults, consider pursuing more advanced medical training from your local fire department or college campus. One of the best courses for someone preparing for a natural disaster is a wilderness medical course, offered by a number of national organizations such as NOLS or international organizations like Remote Medicine International.

For our town, we're recruiting residents to complete Wilderness First Responder training (a two week intensive) in cohorts of about 25 people twice per year. With a long-term view, we'll be able to build up a small army of appropriately trained folks located all over our town who can offer their medical services at our Hubs after a large natural disaster.

As part of your medical preparations, consider augmenting your store-bought first aid kit with additional trauma pads, athletic tape (to hold those larger trauma pads in place), Celox (a granular chemical that both stops bleeding and closes wounds), a suture kit, and several tourniquets. Given our usage scenario will likely contain multiple injured parties, stocking multiple tourniquets will enable you to help more than one person at a time. Look at the RAT model for youth/adults; CAT model for adults. Assume that any first aid kit you purchase will need to have at least 50% of it tailored to your specific needs.

Pain management is a hot topic when you consider pharmacies will be emptied within the first few days of a natural disaster. Think through your preferred types of pain relief and stock up on those items well ahead of time. These items typically come with a very long shelf life.

Kids, Too!

Broadening our skills is the opposite of what many of us were encouraged to do in our youth. We were taught to specialize in order to maximize our salaries (in order to buy more stuff). But it might be wiser to pursue a wide range of shallow/medium skills than deep knowledge of a single skill, especially when working through something as complex and all-encompassing as a wide-scale emergency. We've seen resilience build when the skills in the collective "toolbox" are of a depth beyond what a Google search will teach you, but far less than a black belt in Aikido.

Learning new preparedness skills is not just for adults. Our federal government has created a child-appropriate set of training tools related to preparedness that can have benefits in nonemergency times as well. At the government's Ready.gov website, you can pull down a number of games and educational tools segmented to be appropriate for various ages of children and youth. Reactions to disasters for most children are usually brief but it's important for parents and caregivers to be prepared to help children cope with not only the immediate physical exposure to the disaster but also the ongoing psychological effects of stress after the event. Keep in mind that even if you don't have children of your own, you could easily find yourself in charge of your neighbors' children for days to weeks.

Students of all ages can learn about emergencies and how to prepare for them. Ready.gov curriculum modules based on grade, lead students through exercises and discussions designed to strengthen their "investigative, creative, and communication skills, working both individually and collaboratively." I've reviewed and tested each of the Ready.gov modules; they are worth your time.

Of course, students can also learn homesteading skills. My own children tend to gravitate naturally towards whatever outdoor project my wife and I happen to be working on. They are naturally absorbing best practices from our homesteading experiments for everything, from harvesting rainwater to the travails of moving asparagus (don't move it; pick a permanent spot for asparagus to thrive in for 20 years).

Building Strong Communities

There are many ways to build strong communities that are better able to withstand and recovery from major disasters. They range from the simple to the complex, and from those requiring the skills you already have to skills you'll have to work to acquire.

A simple way to begin that requires little more than the willingness to meet and work with your neighbors is barter. Barter is a way a group of friends or neighbors can share their skills and knowledge with each other, making the entire community stronger. Locally, we have a Time Bank to facilitate these cashless exchanges. It allows members to give services in exchange for credits, which can then be redeemed with other members. Everything is tracked by easy-to-use software, which also allows easy browsing of the other services available from neighbors. Time Banks are different from direct trading and promote a positive upward spiral of giving and receiving.

Community Emergency Response Team

As we've discussed, emergency response training in a variety of areas is not something we need to pursue individually. Like most of everything else, this is better done with neighbors. The nationwide system of Community Emergency Response Team (CERT) demonstrates why this is true.

The ability to work as a team will be crucial as access to fossil fuels and the basics of life like food, water, and shelter become scarce after a natural disaster. Although some strong voices advocate preparing for a wide-scale emergency by moving far away from "civilization" and prying eyes, for most North Americans the opposite will be true. My family and friends plan to stay and help when a national emergency hits, not run away from it. As you read at the beginning of this chapter, that's the conclusion the celebrated journalist Neil Strauss reached in his book *Emergency: This Book Will Save Your Life.*

Like Strauss, I've also undergone CERT training as part of the first CERT team in our county. Going through that training with my friends Russ and Jenni bonded us together not only as a team to support our Fire Department's emergency work but also as local friends building a stronger community.

Created by FEMA and the Department of Homeland Security, CERT is a nationwide program in the United States that educates and trains citizens about disaster preparedness. The education is typically region-specific; we didn't talk much about tornados up here in the Pacific Northwest. The classroom and field training includes basic disaster response in order to support first responders (e.g. fire, police, EMTs). With CERT training, you'll learn basic firefighting, search and rescue, medical triage, and—possibly most important—the incident command system (ICS).

Side note for communication geeks like me: ICS works well and has been proven and honed by preparedness professionals during countless real-world engagements. It allows for clear leadership and communication across the myriad of public and private organizations that will be involved in any large-scale disaster relief effort.

A quick visit to the CERT pages at www.fema.gov will help you find your local CERT program. They have specific programs for campuses, workplaces, and even a special program just for teens. If you don't find a local program, stop by your local fire department with some neighbors and tell them you want to start your own!

Our personal training for emergency preparedness need not be limited to new knowledge. It should also include

getting in shape and maintaining our health. As we discussed in our last chapter, getting in shape in order to be
prepared for emergencies is important. Of course, a healthier version of you provides many dividends for your life in
nonemergency times as well.

I spoke with a local leader in wellness on our island—
Jen Breen, the proprietor of the popular Bainbridge Yoga
House—about the benefits of a healthy mind and spirit for
both individuals and our community. We spoke first of community. Jen observed: "It begins with intention. The most
thriving communities are the ones that begin with a simple
intention, followed by a few people who are attuned to that
same intention. It builds from there—slowly, organically,
and effortlessly."

As I shared with her my work with neighborhoods as a
"sweet spot" between individual homes and larger sections
of the city, she began to nod her head. "If we want our neighborhoods to be real neighborhoods where people on the
same street know one another, help one another and share
with one another, it takes intention," Jen said. "It takes
action and persistence. We need to be willing to reach out
to neighbors to connect, to socialize, and to bridge. If we do
this when times are 'good,' then we have built a powerful
infrastructure that will support us when things fall apart."

We spoke of pursuing wellness and community in the face
of the typical busy, overly-scheduled North American lifestyle. Jen's years of experience in community-building were
evident in her words: "The more isolated, individualized,
and busy we are, the harder it will be for us all when the

rug is taken from underneath—through a tragedy, a natural disaster, or a conflict in the neighborhood. Being friendly and communicative with our neighbors is the simplest route towards healthy communities. Can we offer help? Can we invite them in? Can we solve problems peacefully? Can we offer compassion and generosity to our neighbors, instead of just protecting our own family and acreage? These are the important questions worthy of delving into."

I spoke with another local wellness leader Sal DeRosalia, founder of CrossFit Outcome, about how he has seen his gym improve people's lives and—in addition to getting in shape—how the community he is building improves relationships to make for a stronger community. Sal explained, "I have seen people get through some pretty tough stuff in CrossFit and I don't just mean the workouts. I'm talking about serious stuff like a marriage ending, being laid off, or the passing of a loved one. Our community here was part of the healing process for them. CrossFit, unlike most other gyms I have ever been to, provides that community. We get through these workouts together. We are a band of brothers and sisters that support, cheer and work together to achieve a common goal. We know when someone is having a hard time. Recognizing you have someone who knows you is just about the best thing in the world when you are going through a tough spot."

But developing community can have its challenges. Disagreements happen. Pettiness can arise. When the added significant burden of an emergency is layered on top of already stressed relationships, bad things can happen.

It's important then, to cultivate solid neighborly relationships before the emergency. Jen commented, "By gathering often in the community, comparisons and competitiveness erode from our egos. What's left is a group of people coming together to celebrate one another's uniqueness and what makes us unified as a whole. A community seeks to give people an opportunity to express and offer their gifts. No one leader holds all the responsibility or ownership. A community is about all of its participants, not just a few."

Mentoring

Mentoring is an aspect of community-building that can occur organically or by design. As citizens teach other citizens, new friendships occur and natural mentoring relationships are created. I've collected mentors my whole life, approaching the idea as much as a start-up company approaches the idea of a Board of Directors. Over the past two decades, I've gathered a personal Board of Mentors upon whom I can call when I'm in need of guidance, encouragement, or a sounding board. (You'll hear more from the latest addition to my personal Board, author/activist John Perkins, in the Security chapter.)

Both Jen and Sal have plenty of experience mentoring others via their wellness organizations. But when I asked Sal about examples of the mentoring that happens at CrossFit Outcome, he told me a story that didn't actually include himself. It's a beautiful example of peer mentoring. In Sal's words: "A young woman named Gretchen I've known since she was 10 years old had recently come home after graduating college. She was not quite sure what she was going to do next and was kind of in a funk. On a whim, she decided to visit our gym. After her first class, she said it was the hardest thing she had ever done. But she came back the next day, and the next, and the next."

Sal continued his story: "The class happened to have a few 30-something professional mothers in it. Certainly not of her generation nor a crowd she thought she would become friends with, but the community of women in the class adopted Gretchen and she was quickly their 'girl.' Gretchen bonded with one of these women in particular... Molly. Molly is a wife, a mother of three children—one adopted from Ethiopia—and runs a nonprofit organization that helps underprivileged girls in third world countries. Gretchen and Molly became best of friends. And Gretchen now works with her organization 'Hope By Twelve'."

Molly mentored Gretchen during a time of transition, helping her discover and pursue her vocational passions. Jen has done similar work with countless folks through her yoga studio. Jen said, "At the studio, I've always encouraged people to discover their unique gift and then share it with the community. It's safe, it's embraced, and it's coming from the right place. Participation and full inclusivity are key; less isolation and more togetherness. We know we need community and togetherness to feel fully alive. We thrive on our connections to ourselves, our families, our friends, and communities."

I'm often asked if we plan to move our preparedness and homesteading classes online. While we may eventually add that capability, the primary focus will always remain face-to-face interactions. Through smartphones, computers, and ubiquitous TV screens everywhere in public, we have too much screen time in our lives anyway. We're imparting learning through the classes, while also building the community around a positive, helping perspective of preparedness (rather than one based on fear). This can be done online but is best done in person.

Jen commented on this as well: "Our digital age and the kind of online communities we participate in are just no comparison to or replacement for the ignited energy we feel when we are physically, emotionally, mentally, and soulfully together. While I lived in Mexico, the one thing that I became so enthralled with was the way in which the community flowed: at the town square, in the streets and marketplaces. Babies in arms, uncles and aunts, grandparents, teenagers, abled or disabled—everyone came together daily. I watched them talking, mingling, eating, laughing, praying, dancing. There was a sense of joy I felt as I watched this all unfold on any given day."

Mental and Emotional Resilience

A key aspect of building a strong neighborhood is developing relationships with mental and emotional resilience. While he thinks my permaculture language is a bit weird, Sal gave me a great example of this using what permaculturalists call "stacking function." Normally one would think of exercising as a way to build physical strength. But wellness leaders like Sal know they can layer on additional types of strength through the same workout, beyond just the physical.

Sal explains, "People regularly tell me how much more calm and centered they feel throughout the course of their day as a result of what we do in the gym. CrossFit helps people form a mental toughness as well as alters their perception of what is hard or difficult. I often hear people in our gym say, 'Well, the rest of my day is going to be easy compared to this workout!' If you could do something that was physically, mentally, emotionally, and spiritually beneficial while at the same time the most difficult part of your day, would you do it? If the thing that helped you to lose weight and feel better also made the rest of your day easier, wouldn't you do it?"

Adding new skills to your personal toolbox will certainly be helpful during long emergencies. But the benefits of new knowledge, skills, health, and attitude also can bring us significant joy right here and right now, for our community, our neighbors, and ourselves. By taking action as citizens and learning together as neighbors, we can focus on mutual aid to strengthen our neighborhoods for a more enjoyable life in the future... and today!

Actions: Mutual aid and group resilience is where it's at! Every citizen has unique skills to benefit the neighborhood. What are yours? And how can you add more?

☐ Determine what is your particular passion or interest and master your skill in that area: find classes or instruction you can take yourself or (better yet) with others.

☐ Get emergency medical training: the "Until Help Arrives" and First Aid/CPR programs are a great start.

☐ Augment your first aid kit to fit your (newly expanded) skill set. Plan on needing to attend to multiple trauma incidents throughout your neighborhood in rapid fashion.

☐ Use Ready.gov to provide age-appropriate emergency training to children and youth.

☐ Push for CERT and Wilderness First Responder training in your community through either City Hall or the Fire Department...or both!

☐ Encourage mentoring and emotional support skills as part of the resilience projects within your home and neighborhood.

A FULL PANTRY

BLOCK PARTY

NEIGHBORHOOD WATCH.

SECURITY

A student said to his master: "You teach me fighting, but you talk about peace. How do you reconcile the two?" The master replied: "It is better to be a warrior in a garden than a gardener in a war."

Chinese proverb

In this chapter, we'll discuss security preparations and how they can enhance the sustainability and enjoyment of our everyday lives. Using a broad definition of "security" that includes physical, financial, mental, and relational components, we'll distinguish between one-time procedures that we need to perform immediately after a wide-scale emergency versus ongoing activities that become part of our healthy daily and weekly lifestyle.

A dozen folks of varying ages filtered in through the double doors of Ross' barn just after the dinner hour. Hugs were exchanged among old friends and newcomers were greeted with enthusiastic handshakes. Sam called the session to order.

"Welcome everyone! It's great to see you again. For those of you who were not here last time, we've started this conversation group to share what homesteading projects we've each got going on at each of our places . . . to see how we could help and learn from each other."

Lyla raised her hand and announced: "We've converted the island in our cul-de-sac to food production with our neighbors. It's going well, but we're trying to find a source of manure or compost to put nutrients back into the soil."

Sam responded, "We can help there. We've got a pair of bunnies we call the Manure Machines. You would not believe how much they produce. And it's not 'hot,' so you don't have to compost it. We put it directly on the garden beds and in the fruit tree guilds."

The conversation continued for several hours into the cool night. Topics ranged from a condo's rooftop rainwater harvesting setup to methods of permanently relocating raccoons to protect backyard chickens and outdoor cats.

As folks reluctantly left the meeting at the end of the evening, Ross received extensive thanks for both instigating and hosting the event. He smiled to himself as he closed the barn doors, reflecting on the comments he'd heard about how much more secure folks felt being part of a group like this.

Security Through Community

Immediately after an emergency, our priorities for survival and recovery are (in this order):

1. Rescuing ourselves and those neighbors closest to us,

2. securing shelter from weather and new hazards created by the incident,

3. securing potable water,

4. securing good food.

What happens immediately after an incident is the primary focus of Dr. LuAn Johnson's Map Your Neighborhood (MYN) program. Once this program is set up with your neighbors in advance of a disaster, it will immensely increase your peace of mind or mental security. Dr. Johnson's program teaches you and your neighbors the first nine steps in securing your home and protecting your neighborhood in the event of an earthquake, tornado, or hurricane.

We need to secure ourselves from both the elements (e.g., extreme weather) that likely caused the emergency and any new hazards that have been introduced by the emergency event (e.g., gas leaks, chemical spills, panicked people). It's difficult to think clearly in the aftermath of such a signifi-cant event, so the MYN flip chart you keep under your bed is designed to help you navigate those first few crucial minutes.

The program empowers you to provide physical safety to yourself and your neighbors quickly and efficiently.

The act of reviewing your MYN materials annually with your neighbors also significantly increases your relational security. Our neighborhood has an annual party after the winter holidays as a mechanism to gather ourselves to discuss MYN principles and our specific action plan. By doing so, we are not only updating our flip charts with new skills or tools, we are also deepening our relationships, which lead directly to a more resilient neighborhood.

This emphasis on community is the only positive answer to the question of how to approach the topic of security. Kirsten Bradley and my buddy Nick Ritar run Milkwood, an amazing permaculture educational organization from their base camp at Melliodora in Australia, a beautiful permaculture homestead designed by the co-originator of permaculture, David Holmgren. Kirsten's note below struck a chord with me as I've found my own responses to audiences in the past few years echoing her grounded and positive sentiments:

So now, when occasionally someone comes up at a course and wants to talk survivalism, I almost want to get specific: "So, like, are we talking about just social upheaval, or economic collapse, or Armageddon, or the full thing where people start to eat each other? Because you'll need a different approach depending on what you're thinking to protect yourself from."

In reality, I don't go there. If my family and I are going

to manifest a thriving future for ourselves and our commu-
nity, I need to compost those kinds of thoughts and regen-
erate them into something useful. I focus on what I can do.
And make sure I keep up with my planting plan.

I think for a moment about how, compared to so many
millions of people on this planet, we live in paradise. Maybe
I should stick to being thankful for that. And building a
kick-ass permaculture farm that can feed useful knowledge
and nourishing food back into my community, no matter
what the future holds.

Self-Defense

Even if you've escaped physical harm during the actual natural disaster, human nature can sometimes turn dark after
an incident occurs. It is worthwhile to think through precautions you can take to remain physically safe and secure from
rioting and other forms of violence. We previously discussed
keeping our bodies in good shape not only to be better prepared to recover from a disaster and help others but also to
better enjoy a daily peaceful life.

Self-defense classes are a great way to increase your physical health as well as your self-confidence. Many martial
arts classes focus on a specific approach, with an attitude
of "my kung-fu is better than yours," but increasingly you
can find mixed martial art classes that borrow the best of
multiple disciplines.

Even better are the public safety seminars these martial

arts teachers usually offer to schools, churches, and the public. These seminars have a specific focus and teach a narrow set of self-defense skills that most citizens can learn in just a few sessions. Although to become truly proficient, you'll want to make a longer-term commitment to not just learning these new skills, but regularly practicing them.

If this sparks an interest in you, you'll serve yourself and your loved ones even better with more training. Books and videos can be useful (I suggest those by Kelly McCann), but take a humorous-but-spot-on warning from the character Kip in *Napoleon Dynamite* not to train for cage fighting by watching YouTube videos. Instead, head to your local dojo for real instruction and full armor/full speed practice under supervision.

Rick DeMile is the founder and head trainer at the Family Martial Arts dojo on our island and has an extensive history with the sport of Mixed Martial Arts (MMA). He is one of several martial arts teachers under whom I've studied, but MMA is my favorite as it pulls the best moves from every discipline under the sun. If it works, it gets pulled into MMA.

I asked Rick about the philosophy behind his dojo and he spoke first about reality: "In many sectors of the martial arts world, training has devolved into a McDojo environment where students are coddled, entertained, and handed a belt no matter what they do or how they perform. Does this have any resemblance to the world in which we live?"

As my instructor, Rick and I have obviously talked extensively about fighting. We've covered just about every aspect of it there is, including quite a bit of time discussing how to avoid a fight in the first place. My sparring partner, author/activist John Perkins, and I approached Rick years ago with a specific request to learn and train both ends of the fighting spectrum, from verbal de-escalation techniques to all the illegal moves not allowed in MMA.

Neither John nor I have any interest in competing in MMA as a sport, but we both find ourselves in situations where we'd like to know hyper-effective street defense moves to protect ourselves and our loved ones. The moves we were interested in were designated illegal in MMA since they would shorten the bouts (longer bouts means better business) and risk immediate/permanent injury to the professional MMA athletes.

Rick even allowed me to introduce the idea of sparring with a live partner (usually John) while holding a half-size training dummy torso. The dummy was the same size as my child and John's grandchild at the time, so the drill was to defuse the situation verbally while scooping up the "child" and exiting the scene. Should the verbal de-escalation not work, the drill turned into using one or more of these street defense moves while protecting the "child." All three of us learned quite a bit during those sessions about the unique aspects of fighting while shielding a loved one.

(By the way, should you ever meet John at one of his many speaking engagements, he is almost a foot taller than I am and has a black belt in Tae Kwon Do—a martial art that emphasizes kicking. I can tell you from experience you do not want to get kicked by his long legs, whether he has his grandchild with him or not!)

But what about taking the practice and mentality behind self-defense skills into the real world which—hopefully—rarely sees a violent encounter? Rick gave me a great example: "Most of us would prefer to avoid a real fight (physical engagement) if at all possible since hurting another person (and let's be honest—getting hurt ourselves) is a repulsive idea. Many 'fight' principles can and should be translated into life principles for the benefit of our students."

Just as we're giving a broad treatment of the word "security," Rick gives a broad definition to "self-defense." He explains, "Most people think 'self-defense' means protecting yourself against physical violence. But this idea has a much broader application that I have thankfully seen accomplished in the lives of so many students over the years. If a person can successfully face and deal with another person trying to punch them in the nose, they can also take that skill and translate it into defending themselves from bullying in school or the workplace."

"A common theme in martial arts training and certainly in a self-defense scenario is the never-give-up mindset. The other day I saw a young female student struggling to accomplish a Brazilian Jiu Jitsu move against a partner who was giving a lot of resistance. The point of the drill was not simply to perform the move successfully, but also to never stop struggling to be successful until the timekeeper called time. That is exactly what she did. When this young lady is faced with a challenging situation in her life somewhere down the road, she'll show the same determination and resolve."

I've experienced the community and strength of relationships that physical training organizations like a dojo can create. Rick and his staff have taken years to build what he calls the "friendship factor". He explains, "As someone who has trained in the martial arts for 40 years, I can certainly say that I have learned many, many techniques. But when I look back over the years, it is not the techniques that stand out. It is the people with whom I have had the privilege of training and learning. I love to see students training together, but it is also extremely satisfying to see them laughing together, struggling together, and developing bonds of friendship which can last a lifetime."

Active Shooter Response

I'm often asked about how to respond to an "active shooter" scenario. While we are all (unfortunately) familiar with these scenarios in schools and houses of worship, it's worth thinking through and understanding the best practices should that scenario ever extend itself to your neighborhood.

FEMA's response guidelines for an active shooter situation include best practices for what to do before, during, and after an incident. Before an incident (think: start on this list tomorrow morning), responsible residents should know their community's response plan, how to apply first aid skills to themselves and others (particularly tourniquets), and develop the habit of identifying both exits and hiding spots in locations they frequent.

I was pleased to see FEMA update their recommendations in recent years for what to do during an incident to include "fight" if the options of "run" and "hide" are not possible. It is important to empower everyone—folks of any age and ability—to know that they do not need to cower as victims. More likely, you will employ more than one of the run-hide-fight options if you find yourself in one of these tragic scenarios.

Finally, note the importance of follow-up after you've exited an active shooter scenario. Once you've reached a safe location, seeking medical attention for yourself or providing it to others is paramount. Once life-threatening injuries have been dealt with, be sure to seek professional help to work through the psychological, emotional, and spiritual ramifications of surviving such an ordeal.

Armed Defense

I happen to be "firearms agnostic," but the topic of weaponry must be considered and discussed by all North Americans, as access to firearms in our country is ubiquitous. As an exurban micro-farmer, I have a love/hate relationship with deer, coyotes, and raccoons. I appreciate their beauty and role in our ecosystem, but I'm more than a little frustrated by their destruction and attacks on my neighborhood's pets, livestock, and crops. I've discussed this with a multitude of professional farmers and ranchers across the country, and most (but definitely not all) consider a firearm to be an essential piece of farm equipment, particularly in areas with rampant deer and larger predators.

But the use of firearms when discussing security is not limited to dealing with wild animals threatening our food-stuffs and livestock. When thinking about long emergencies, it does no good to grow your own food and raise your own animals only to have them taken away by the first thug coming off the highway who has a gun.

I spoke with Alan Kasper about the Bainbridge Island Sportsmen's Club, where he serves as both the President and as one of the certified Range Safety Officers. The club is a historical site, and in addition to hosting community activities like holiday dinners for island seniors, it provides a safe environment for practice with firearms and archery. Alan told me about his observation of families at the pistol and archery ranges enjoying afternoons of target practice together. Regardless of how you feel about this political "hot potato" topic, if you are going to include firearms in your life, you absolutely MUST get safety training from professionals that includes handling and storage.

Alan commented, "Our safety officers teach safety in all aspects of the sports we pursue. We teach mental discipline and focus, for one cannot shoot firearms or archery equipment safely without keen focus. Our sport develops hand-eye coordination and instills responsibility of handling firearms and archery equipment, which, if used irresponsibly can cause damage, not unlike a car. We also help prepare individuals who are going to be using firearms or archery equipment for hunting. Whether using a bow or firearm for hunting or self-defense, one must conduct oneself in a safe and responsible manner. The old adage of "practice makes perfect" is true. This requires familiarity, practice, discipline, and respect."

In 2007, a blog post by author Marko Kloos titled *Why the Gun is Civilization* began circulating on the internet. I'm presenting his brief words here as a summary of what I've heard for years from so many owners of firearms:

Human beings only have two ways to deal with one another: reason and force. If you want me to do something for you, you have a choice of either convincing me via argument, or force me to do your bidding under threat of force. Every human interaction falls into one of those two categories, without exception. Reason or force, that's it.

In a truly moral and civilized society, people exclusively interact through persuasion. Force has no place as a valid method of social interaction, and the only thing that removes force from the menu is the personal firearm, as paradoxical as it may sound to some.

When I carry a gun, you cannot deal with me by force. You have to use reason and try to persuade me, because I have a way to negate your threat or employment of force. The gun is the only personal weapon that puts a 100-pound woman on equal footing with a 220-pound mugger, a 75-year old retiree on equal footing with a 19-year old gangbanger, and a single gay guy on equal footing with a carload of drunk guys with baseball bats. The gun removes the disparity in physical strength, size, or numbers between a potential attacker and a defender.

There are plenty of people who consider the gun as the source of bad force equations. These are the people who think that we'd be more civilized if all guns were removed from society, because a firearm makes it easier for a mugger to do his job. That, of course, is only true if the mugger's potential victims are mostly disarmed either by choice or by legislative fiat—it has no validity when most of a mugger's potential marks are armed. People who argue for the banning of arms ask for automatic rule by the young, the strong, and the many, and that's the exact opposite of a civilized society. A mugger, even an armed one, can only make a successful living in a society where the state has granted him a force monopoly.

Then there's the argument that the gun makes confrontations lethal that otherwise would only result in injury. This argument is fallacious in several ways. Without guns involved, confrontations are won by the physically superior party inflicting overwhelming injury on the loser. People who think that fists, bats, sticks, or stones don't constitute lethal force watch too much TV, where people take beatings and come out of it with a bloody lip at worst. The fact that the gun makes lethal force easier works solely in favor of the weaker defender, not the stronger attacker. If both are armed, the field is level. The gun is the only weapon that's as lethal in the hands of an octogenarian as it is in the hands of a weightlifter. It simply wouldn't work as well as a force equalizer if it wasn't both lethal and easily employable.

When I carry a gun, I don't do so because I am looking for a fight, but because I'm looking to be left alone. The gun *at my side means that I cannot be forced, only persuaded. I don't carry it because I'm afraid, but because it enables me to be unafraid. It doesn't limit the actions of those who would interact with me through reason, only the actions of those who would do so by force. It removes force from the equation...and that's why carrying a gun is a civilized act.*

Mental & Emotional Discipline

Being truly secure means developing the ability to turn first to ourselves as a source of mental and emotional strength. We become better citizens and neighbors when we exercise self-care of our bodies and minds. Exercising self-care now will benefit us later, whether it is developing physical strength to push through a short-term crisis, or creating mental stamina to endure the daily struggle of simply getting out of bed during a months-long emergency. It behooves us to develop mental toughness and flexibility. In both emergencies and in regular life, having a mind that is supple and strong—like tall bamboo in high winds—is a desirable goal.

When we look at the topic of security holistically, we can see how positive preparations in these different aspects can lead to better humans, better neighborhoods, better towns, and a better society.

I spoke with author/activist John Perkins while he was traveling through Costa Rica. Our conversation quickly went from the physical security measures we have to endure when traveling to a global view of security. We discussed changing not only the mental outlook of citizens but also the outlook of our larger organizations, be they corporate or government.

Here's John: "Security takes on new meaning during this time of severe financial, political, social, and environmental turmoil. Every time I go through the security checkpoints at airports I wonder at the fallacy of the process. As a martial artist, I know my hands are more lethal than a tube of toothpaste. I also know that any professional bad guy can get a polymer gun or knife through those machines. As a society, we need to redefine security. It is no longer about protecting ourselves from men in Himalayan caves or on Somali fishing boats. It is about getting both business and government to understand that their job is to create a sustainable, just, peaceful world, where future generations of all species can thrive."

As we were signing off before he was about to enter another security zone, John left me with these encouraging words, "There will always be a few crazies around. But if we take away the causes of desperation and anger that fuel them, peace and security will follow."

Financial Security

As John explained, our corporations certainly can (must!) play a role in making our society safe and secure. But as responsible citizens, it also behooves us to make our own financial contingency plans. We must redefine "job security" and "wealth" from the classic definitions to something more resilient, something like a strong network of relationships on which you can depend.

It's a conversation that many Americans don't like to have, but we all have way too much debt in our lives from living too far above our means. I've recommended Dave Ramsey's books and seminars to countless folks interested in taking back control of their finances in order to bring more security to their lives. It's a simple, straightforward approach to living within your means, eliminating debt, and building up an emergency fund. As Ramsey often quips, he's just recommending the same advice you would receive from your grandmother.

I know several families who have followed Ramsey's "advice from grandmother" for years and now enjoy debt-free living. For my family, this has made all the difference in the world when moving in parallel paths towards both simplicity and preparedness. But I've also experienced the awkwardness of this financial conversation centered on excessive debt with many others. I've often wondered why we don't talk more about this, both as families and in the general American public dialogue.

I asked writer Joshua Becker about this and how as a community we can pull a judo move to flip the topic on its head. How can we go from being awkward and silent on the subject to having an attitude of openness and camaraderie? He's written about this exact topic, so he had numbers at the tip of his tongue, "The statistics concerning our personal financial habits are downright sad: one in four Americans have no savings; 57 percent of American households have no budget; the average U.S. household debt is 136 percent of household income, and money often ranks as the #1 source of conflict in marriages. And yet, nobody is asking for help."

So why aren't we more frank about finances with close family and friends, especially when so many of us are drowning in debt? Why do we actively avoid or ignore the topic instead of seeking help, either from professionals or even just from respected friends? What would it look like if we could create a positive culture of frugality, where it becomes cooler to wear used items from the thrift shop than brand new apparel?

Joshua replied, "It can be a very humbling process to ask for help—especially if we think everyone else has it all figured out. And when it comes to money, there is definitely a large percentage of the population putting up a false front that everything is just fine. If your spending habits are not working for you, know that you are not alone. Know that many Americans struggle with the exact same problem. This realization won't eliminate the stress of living in debt or living paycheck-to-paycheck. But it should provide you with the motivation to bring up the conversation with someone you trust. Start with this, "Hey, can I ask you a question about money?"

If you have already started down this path of simplification and debt elimination, I'd encourage you to discover the treasure trove of information on Chris Martenson's Peak Prosperity website. Much of it is biased towards action (my favorite kind of information) and includes a savvy investment guide section.

The Security of Helpful Neighbors

When asked about our local resilience groups—what they are and what they do—my quick answer is that we encourage neighbors to help neighbors. The creation and maintenance of solid friendships are significantly more important than any other type of emergency preparation you may make. Let me say that one more time for emphasis: more than any other preparation you can perform, or piece of gear you can buy, creating a network of caring relationships with others in your immediate area (not across town) is the single most important type of security preparation you can make. Many of the folks I know who are more focused on self-sufficiency than building group resilience think that statement to be heresy, but there are other thought leaders who would agree with me.

Joel Skousen has written and consulted extensively on the design of secure homes. He has researched the best locations to endure emergencies following both natural and human-made disasters. He has documented how to fortify one's current location to stay safer according to the potential disasters in your bioregion. As an architect and contractor, Skousen clearly knows what he is doing and has decades of hands-on experience. But I find it most encouraging that this expert on physical security has this to say about preparedness: "Possessing a few personal friends you can intrinsically trust at all times is one of the most important contingency preparations you can make."

Over several months, I discussed the importance of

relationships with Chuck Collins, a senior scholar at the Institute for Policy Studies (IPS) and co-creator of Resilience Circles (aka Common Security Clubs). Resilience Circles are small groups of proactive people increasing their personal security through learning, mutual aid, social action, and community support. As I shared early writings of this book with him, I found Chuck's insight most helpful: "Many people are trying to face the new ecological and economic future but find they cannot do it in isolation. There is only so much troubling information we can take in without some sense of urgency and ability to make a difference. There are also limits—as you point out in your book—to individual solutions. We have to prepare at the community level."

We talked about the genesis of the Resilience Circles project—which has spread nationwide—and its purpose. Chuck explained, "Resilience Circles are a way people can begin to connect with others, learn together, and strengthen personal and community resilience. Think of them as support groups for neighborhood preparation at the block level. Most Resilience Circles are 8-15 people who have some common affinity; they are members of a religious congregation, are physical neighbors, or share some other bond. They meet regularly to strengthen mutual aid and figure out meaningful actions they can take together."

Building resilience in small groups and large, street by street in neighborhoods and across small towns is clearly the best way to build real security. Common among the various definitions of security—from physical to mental, emotional to spiritual—is the core of relationships, relationships with our neighbors and our planet. More wisdom from Chuck: "Real security can only be found in the strength of our communities. What makes us secure is a sense that we are being held by our friends and neighbors, that we will have networks to fall back on and to help one another."

When tragic security-related incidents like bombings occur, we are reminded of the immeasurable value of those around us. Current government response to these incidents does not seem to be curtailing future tragedies, although to be fair the behemoth does appear to be slowly awakening: look up the excellent *Foreign Policy* (foreignpolicy.com) article on why walkable communities, sustainable economics, and multilateral diplomacy are the future of American power.

If we, as citizens, can work ahead of the tragedy, ahead of the violence, to help others—particularly those with unstable mental faculties—we may be able to stem off their violent behavior. By helping those individuals who wish violence upon their communities to better connect with their neighbors and other loving community members, we can see the truism in the words of Dr. Martin Luther King, Jr.: "Hate cannot drive out hate, only love can do that."

Actions: Using a broad definition of "security" that includes physical, financial, mental, and emotional components, actions taken here can enhance of our everyday lives.

☐ Consider both being mentored by someone you respect as well as mentoring someone else.

☐ Self-defense: pursue a form of self-defense training most appropriate for yourself and your loved ones, for physical and mental fitness as well as confidence.

☐ Create patterns of self-discipline to secure your family's financial security. Know that it is always OK to ask for outside help from expert sources like Dave Ramsey and in-person encouragement from Resilience Circles.

☐ Speaking of which, create and maintain a local Resilience Circle to develop closer relationships in your immediate neighborhood.

INDIVIDUALS.

GROUPS.

COMMUNITIES.

OPT OUT TO OPT IN

"We ask for too much salvation by legislation. All we need to do is empower individuals with the right philosophy and the right information to opt out en masse."

Joel Salatin
Author, speaker, and farmer

Citizens can opt into positive solutions while opting out of soul-deadening activities that do not serve to better themselves and their communities. Neighbors can take the initiative to create significant opportunities for themselves and those around them to not only survive the initial shock of an emergency but to also quickly bounce back and thrive on the other side of it.

Ross and Bill were working on a project together. The band saw quieted down and both men removed their ear protection to continue the conversation. Their construction project of two new beehives for the roof of their apartment building was going well.

"So how was Salatin's talk?" Bill asked.

Ross answered, "That guy is an infectious speaker, to be sure. I'm still thinking about how to apply what his farm does with chicken tractors. With a few modifications, we could adapt his approach to that vacant lot a block over."

"You thinking more in the style of Andy Lee, with low voltage electrified fencing so you don't have to move them every day?"

"Yeah, I think so. Joel talked about how Andy had studied his methods and offered improvements. But the main thing that struck me from Joel's talk was when he responded to a question from one of our city council people. Joel said, 'We ask for too much salvation by legislation. All we need to do is empower individuals with the right philosophy and the right information to opt out en masse.' I like that phrase: 'opting out en masse.' That feels like what our little group of homesteading friends here in our section of town are doing."

"I completely agree," replied Bill, "and it feels like it's spreading to other sustainability-minded groups around here. This feels like we're building real resilience into our town."

Opportunities for Greatness

As we pursue building resilience into our neighborhoods, we need to create space in our lives to do so. Since there are only so many hours in a day, for every project or relationship that we begin, we need to opt out of a different one.

By opting out en masse, I'm proposing a mass exodus of thoughtful, positive and grounded people from a worldview that consuming more and more is a constitutional right. Opting out does not mean we go into hiding and begin hoarding foodstuffs. It does not mean heading off to the hills to build a survivalist bunker. As John Robb of Resilient Communities explains, "If you live in a home and community that is resilient, the future isn't a threat. Just the opposite. It's an opportunity for personal and community greatness and not something merely to be survived with canned goods and bottled water. It's a pathway to a deeply meaningful and abundant life for you, your family, your neighbors, and everyone in the world that wants to connect with you as a peer."

Opting out means making space to engage more deeply in things that matter by divorcing ourselves from things that don't, like reality TV shows, the rat race, addictive hits of fat and sugar in fast food, keeping up the with Joneses, social media, or overscheduling our kids so their life is a blur and ours is spent shuttling them around. By opting out, we create room in our lives to opt into new things.

Once we've created space, we can opt in to new things that create value and resilience in our lives. Things like participating in your local farmer's market, joining your town's watershed council to clean up waterways, creating a new group to promote money-saving energy retrofits for homes, volunteering with your Zero Waste initiative, or helping others through your local social justice nonprofit.

Who You Spend Time With

Personally, keeping an "opt out" perspective the last five years has also changed how I pursue and maintain new relationships. In my 20s and 30s, I valued white-collar jobs and, as an extension, white collar friends. I certainly had close friends who did not hold white-collar jobs, but I failed to appreciate them or prioritize spending time with them.

While high tech marketing gurus are fun to hang out with at industry events, they're (usually) not very useful in an emergency situation as they have very little "real life" skills. Since I began prioritizing permaculture and preparedness in my personal life, I've purposely sought out a new set of friends—irrigation experts, master carpenters, farmers, electricians, etc.—that I enjoy, both for their camaraderie and for the skills I learn from them when we work on projects together. Not only do I get to count them as friends during good times, but I know they'll stand with me during bad times, too. They'll be working beside me as sisters and brothers as we put our community back together after a major disaster.

As the infamous motivational speaker Jim Rohn often

quipped, you are the average of the five people with whom you spend the most time. But this wisdom is nothing new. The person who likely inspired the phrase "Renaissance Man," Johann Wolfgang von Goethe, stated about 200 years ago, "Tell me with whom you consort and I will tell you who you are." Consider this when deciding with whom you want to invest some of your newly found "opt in" time.

As a community, we can opt into positive, solution-seeking thinking and plan to handle the emergencies our city may face in the near future. Some disasters are certain; it's only a matter of time before the next significant earthquake or severe winter storm hits our Pacific Northwest island. Others—whether natural disasters or human-made catastrophes like a terrorist attack, nuclear accident, or economic meltdown—can still be anticipated in a general sense. Neighborhoods that have taken the initiative to opt in to the positive activities we've discussed in this book will have a significant advantage in both survival and achieving a swift recovery.

Where Are You on Your Journey?

"Awareness arrives in stages" is one of my favorite phrases from author James Kunstler because it passes the reality test every week in conversations I have with folks both local and abroad. In my own life, awareness of sustainability issues came in waves. First, it was organic food when my children were born, then the social justice aspects of Fair

Trade products, then green cleaning/building products for the home to keep everyone healthy, and then energy-related aspects of climate change and Peak Oil.

I've now found a useful corollary to Kunstler's phrase from economic researcher Chris Martenson, who urges us to consider not how we will survive the coming emergency, but what our lives will look like on the other side of it. He points to the importance of developing a strong and healthy community now. What kind of people do we want as neighbors after a transition period to a slower, more austere pace of life? The answer to that question gives us the incentive to build those relationships now.

Whether gradual or sudden, this change in our attitude towards opting out of destructive practices and opting into life-affirming ones is important. Another conversation with author/activist John Perkins revealed this wisdom: "The solution—and the opportunity—is our evolution into a new, more conscious species. We live in the wealthiest country in history but also the one with the highest rates of murder, drug abuse, and incarceration. So the message is clear: We must change our mindset."

We went deeper into the conversation, with me trying to get at exactly what and how our mindsets must change. John explained, "This is an important watershed moment in human evolution. It is about neighborhoods, and even more importantly, it is about that bigger idea of resilience. Young people around the world understand, as previous generations never did, the importance of recognizing that for the first time in human history, we ALL face the same crises.

And because we are ALL communicating with each other, books like *Prepared Neighborhoods* are part of the solution. We must gain a new perspective on what it is to be human in a tiny space station that has no shuttles to use when the going gets tough. We are all in this together. Community, today, is both hyper-local AND global."

Making Change En Masse

This focus on empowering neighborhoods and communities is important to feed into the positive systemic thinking that we must bring to our culture. This is the "en masse" aspect of opting out. It refers to our planet's desperate need for humans to create positive systemic change in business, education, food production, and more. Each are powerful forces that contribute to climate change, particularly our carbon footprint as a species, and the acidification of our oceans.

Toby Hemenway is one of the founding minds behind permaculture, an approach to food production that eschews the reliance on oil and chemicals. I've enjoyed the "big picture" thinking behind his essays in recent years before he passed away. One essay in particular on nomads and the culture of fear we've created with our farm-based civilization is controversial and thought-provoking.

Hemenway writes,

"Can a farming civilization ever stop being afraid? Only if it is no longer brainwashed into the belief that domination,

labor, and order are what protect it from the caprices of an untrustable nature. Can it ever allow other cultures to exist alongside it? I'm not sure. I have a vision of farmers living only where farming has proven to be more or less sustainable, in large river valleys like the Nile and Mississippi, while nomads, foragers, and some horticulturists live in the hills, the smaller valleys, and the delicate lands that agriculture can only destroy.

But that would demand that those farmers not fear the freedom of the nomads and, so far, that hasn't happened. I hope we can mature to that point. I wish someday the descendants of Sitting Bull, as well as mine, can ride again across unfenced plains to hunt bison and gather in transient villages along the Little Bighorn and anywhere.

My wife and I are not true nomads and couldn't ever be. Those days died in 1876. Our nomadism relied on fossil fuels, landlords with furnished rentals, farmers to sell us food, and the whole bloody infrastructure of civilization. I have no illusions about whose shoulders—and corpses—I'm standing on.

But I've now had the chance to stretch my leash far enough to glimpse the larger features of a culture grounded in fear-mongering and violence, whose very laws, values, work ethic, and traditions enshrine the domination of the many by the powerful few. That is a culture that is killing a planet."

One of the best minds writing about the systemic change that we must bring about in the realm of business is David

Korten, who also happens to live on our island with his wife Fran, the publisher of '*YES! Magazine*'. In his book titled '*The Great Turning*,' David writes about the importance of transforming our largest economic institutions. One passage, in particular, appealed to the permaculturalist in me. David writes,

"*I still struggled, however, with how best to advance the transition from a corporate-led global economy to a planetary system of community-led local living economies. At the beginning of 2001, I attended an invitational consultation at the Esalen Institute at which both Elisabet Sahtouris, an evolution biologist, and Janine Benyus, a biological scientist and a leading proponent of biomimicry, made presentations.*

Both noted that the processes of natural succession by which forest ecosystems evolve offer a potential model for economic transformation. The earliest, colonizing stage of forest-system development is dominated by fast-growing, aggressively competitive, and transient species that are eventually displaced by the emergence of the more patient, cooperative, settled, energy-efficient species that define the mature phase.

This model pointed to a strategy of change through emergence and displacement. These living system concepts defined the underlying strategic premise of the Business Alliance for Local Living Economies (BALLE), which was cofounded that same year by Laury Hammel and Judy Wicks, two visionary entrepreneurs with a passionate commitment to the idea that the proper defining purpose of business is to serve life and community."

And 'community' is the key! As another Seattleite Jim Diers explains in his *Neighbor Power* book—an excellent resource for community building—citizens are empowered and communities are developed when participatory economics and democracy are pursued at the level below that of a city but above that of a single family. Once again we find ourselves at the sweet spot of the neighborhood!

Plan for the Future but Live in the Now

There are three distinct benefits to developing close social ties with neighbors related to natural disasters: before, immediately after, and beyond—during the months/years of recovery. We've discussed the many benefits of neighborly relations prior to a large-scale emergency. And we've also covered the benefits of a Map Your Neighborhood program for bringing mutual aid to those nearest to you.

Let's now talk for a moment about the importance of neighborhoods and neighbors in the long months and years of recovery post-incident. We've recently learned that social ties with neighbors and friends are crucial during the time of recovery after the disaster has passed. Professor Ichiro Kawachi, an epidemiologist at Harvard's School of Public Health, studied the aftereffects of the Japanese tsunami.

Professor Kawachi and his team found that when social

ties were not preserved, and survivors lost contact with neighbors, a significant increase in dementia and loss of physical function occurred. The professor noted in his report, "An under-appreciated aspect of disaster policy is that human relations matter as much as giving out timely aid."

Although no one can foresee the exact future, we would be wise to plan with our neighbors for future disasters that are inevitable, both natural and manmade. Although we can be optimistic about some possibilities, such as the near limitless clean energy from a serious societal investment in geothermal, wind, and solar, we should also be realistic in planning for more negative eventualities, such as a pandemic flu "correcting" our overpopulated areas. Nevertheless, it behooves us to keep our general outlook positive and focused on living the best life we can, day by day, for ourselves, our loved ones, and our neighbors.

As Neil Strauss reminds us in his book *Emergency*, we'll do well to remember the ancient parting words of Fishwife Sidur to Gilagamesh: "Each day, wash your head, bathe your body, and wear clothes that are sparkling fresh. Fill your stomach with tasty food. Play, sing, dance, and be happy both day and night. Delight in the pleasures that your wife brings you, and cherish the little child who holds your hand. Make every day of your life a feast of rejoicing!"

We can view natural disasters and the anticipation of them through a positive lens if we so choose, enabling us to focus on the opportunities. The opportunities for a greater community, deeper relationships, and corrected life priorities cannot be denied. We each decide every day through what lens we shall look at life and what story we create with ourselves and others. Let's collectively choose a positive lens and a story based on love rather than fear. Let's pursue resilience together!

Please join our conversation online at preparedneighborhoods.com.

APPENDIX A:
SHELTER-IN-PLACE CHECKLIST

This Shelter-in-Place list can be used for an individual household or (my strong preference) extended to include select neighbors to take advantage of bulk purchases, sharing of tools, and the many other benefits of a strong neighborhood discussed in the book. Most North Americans certainly do not need to buy more stuff! Instead, we'd do well to reimagine additional uses of our existing possessions for mutual aid, particularly when considered as part of a shared set of materials with neighbors.

It should be augmented to last you and your loved ones a minimum of 14 days; more if you expect to be housing additional guests or know of specific natural disasters common to your region. Related but separate is the accompanying Get Home Bag list, designed for just enough time to return home assuming normal commute vehicles/avenues are not available (less than 48 hours), and Go Bag list, a bag kept packed and ready at hand for a three-day evacuation (double check that assumption for your specific area).

Since they are likely stored at your home, your Go Bags are part of your Shelter-in-Place kit. While you do not need to duplicate gear purchases for both, keep in mind the wisdom of redundancy, "Two is one; one is none," when considering key items that could make life difficult if they were lost or broken without an available replacement (e.g. a can opener).

For all items consider a 14-day minimum supply, more if you live in a remote or hard-to-reach area (e.g. an island). Many daily-use items such as rain gear or sun hats are not included on this list; they are assumed to be already in your place of residence and in good working order.

☐ Water: two gallons per person, per day. If you have pets or other domestic animals, take note of their normal water needs and add that to your water storage.

☐ Multi-person water filter such as the Big Berkey system.

☐ LifeStraw, Sawyer filter, or other personal water purification gear. Water purification tablets may be preferred.

☐ Food: non-perishable, easy-to-prepare items that do not require refrigeration. Include food for your pets and domestic animals, too.

☐ Flashlights: two per person (one large, one small) with batteries stored outside of the units. Consider at least one headlamp per person for hands-free operation.

☐ Extra batteries.

☐ Battery-powered, solar, or hand-crank NOAA weather radio.

☐ Prescription medications and scrips to secure more.

☐ Backup assistive devices such as glasses, contact lenses/solutions, and hearing aids (with batteries).

☐ First aid kit, augmented with additional trauma pads, Celox, athletic tape, suture kit, and a practical instruction manual.

☐ P100 masks and additional daily replacement filters. I like the both the 3M 7500 Half Face Piece Respirator and 3M 8293 P100 Disposable Particulate Respirator products.

☐ Clear plastic sheeting, larger trash bags, and duct tape for sanitation and weather protection (i.e. covering broken windows).

☐ Personal hygiene items (e.g. menstrual products, soap, hand sanitizer, moist towelettes, toothpaste).

☐ Five-gallon bucket with snap-on toilet lid and optional deodorant.

☐ Toilet paper and large trash bag of sawdust for your five-gallon bucket or pit latrine.

☐ Potable water purification tablets (my preference) or unscented chlorine bleach (does not kill Giardia) or Betadine antiseptic solution (does not kill Cryptosporidium) and rubber gloves for sterilization and cleansing. For the liquid solutions, duct tape a medicine dropper to the bottle. Consider an alternative non-allergen antiseptic to Betadine if appropriate for your loved ones.

☐ Extra sunscreen and bug spray if those are an issue in your bioregion.

☐ Pocket multi-tool with knife.

☐ Hand tools for dealing with rubble and debris: multi-purpose folding shovel, 18" or longer pry bar, long-handled ax, wire saw, and work gloves for each person in the household.

☐ Small fireproof/waterproof safe that contains extra cash in small bills, an extra set of car keys and house keys, and a binder with copies of personal documents, including pertinent medical information, proof of address, deed/lease to home, passports, birth certificates, insurance policies, financial/payment records, driver's license, family reunification plans, emergency contact information, etc.

☐ Standard charger(s) for your cell phone(s) and other small electronic devices.

☐ Solar-powered charger with generic USB output for all your small electronic devices.

☐ Emergency blankets such as Heat Sheets or survival bags (two per person), extra blankets, and standard mummy sleeping bags

☐ Two-way radios (FRS or GMRS) and the instruction manual. Store batteries outside of the units themselves. Preferred alternative would be a Ham radio if you've secured your license, however, also keep in mind the communication needs of loved ones who do not have a Ham radio license.

☐ Under-the-bed items (per your Map Your Neighborhood flipchart): signal whistle, hardhat, headlamp with fresh batteries, sturdy shoes, fire mask (sometimes called an oxygen hood), fire extinguisher, and your MYN flipchart itself, of course!

☐ Ability to cook food assuming your normal methods are inaccessible: waterproof matches, lighters, camp stove, extra fuel canisters, and appropriately sized cooking pots for your camp stove.

☐ Any tools/supplies you deem necessary to secure your home.

☐ Wrenches and pliers (or purpose-built tool)

appropriately sized to shut off your utilities. Best practice: duct tape these tools directly to the meters that need to be shut off.

☐ Camping tent (does not need to be a lightweight backpacking version) that includes a rain fly and ground tarp. If you already have a tent, be sure it includes a rain fly.

☐ Tarps plus rope or paracord to create temporary overhead protection.

Next, pause for a moment to consider any additional special needs for each and every member of your household, including pets. Make note of unusual resources you regularly purchase for these individuals (e.g. diapers). Write those items here:

☐ _____

☐ _____

☐ _____

☐ _____

☐ _____

And finally, take a moment to review the accompanying Go Bag list for additional ideas you may want to also include in your Shelter-in-Place list.

Whew! That's quite the list! To reiterate, this list can be used for an individual household, or (my preference) extended to include select neighbors. Leverage the good neighbor relationships you are building; many hands make for a lighter (and less expensive) load!

APPENDIX B:
GO BAG CHECKLIST

Make notes directly on this list for required items specific to you and your loved ones, such as medicines, assistive devices (e.g. eyeglasses), and regional-specific gear (e.g. a sun hat for desert dwellers, rain gear for folks in the Pacific Northwest). Also, consider any regional-specific natural disasters you may encounter and add those to your list (e.g. swim goggles and P100 breath masks if you'll be sheltering-in-place after a volcanic eruption).

Each member of your household should have a Go Bag, including pets. Balance loads for weight and content across all bags (e.g. don't place 100% of the food in a single Go Bag). After you've assembled your Go Bag, take photos of each bag with its contents nearby. Laminate these photos for easy reference later as to what is in each bag. Remember that your Go Bag contents count for the same items in your Shelter-in-Place checklist if stored in the same location.

☐ Duffel bag or large backpack to hold items.

☐ Water: two gallons per person per day; 3-day supply for evacuation or (much easier) the ability the **make** your own water supply via a purification method of your choice such as purification tablets or a small hand pump.

☐ Food: 3-day supply of non-perishable, nutrient dense food for evacuation (energy bars).

☐ Manual can opener if applicable.

☐ Backpacking stove with cook set, utensils, and fuel canisters.

☐ Battery-powered or hand crank NOAA Weather Radio with tone alert.

☐ Ham, FRS or GMRS radio with instruction manual.

☐ Two flashlights (one handheld, one headlamp) with extra batteries stored exterior to flashlight.

☐ Small first aid kit, supplemented with Celox, trauma pads, athletic tape, suture kit, Betadine or alternative non-allergen antiseptic, and disposable gloves.

☐ Signal whistle.

☐ Lighter or waterproof matches.

☐ P100 masks and additional daily replacement filters; I like the both the 3M 7500 Half Face Piece Respirator and 3M 8293 P100 Disposable Particulate Respirator products

☐ Medications (minimum of 7-day supply in case your three-day evacuation does not go according to plan).

☐ Glasses, contact lenses with solution, hearing aids with backup batteries.

☐ Personal hygiene and comfort items: menstrual products, lip balm, pain relievers.

☐ Sanitation: toilet paper, moist towelettes, two large garbage bags, five large Ziploc bags, and plastic ties.

☐ Pocket multi-tool with knife.

☐ Work gloves.

☐ Folding multi-tool shovel/saw (many models will include a compass).

☐ Cell phone with chargers, battery backup, and/or solar charger.

☐ Survival sleeping bag or two Heat Sheet blankets plus duct tape to make your own emergency version bag; avoid the ubiquitous and ineffective Mylar blankets.

☐ Tarp with 100' paracord to secure it, or tent, and second ground tarp.

☐ Sturdy shoes.

☐ Complete change of sturdy clothing including a long-sleeved shirt, long pants.

☐ Two pairs of hiking socks.

☐ Eye protection: sunglasses, safety goggles, and hat.

☐ Appropriate weather protection: rain poncho or shell jacket, sunscreen, cold weather jacket.

☐ Regional map with reunification location(s) and possible evacuation routes marked.

☐ Notebook and pencil.

☐ Sillcock key to access water from commercial buildings.

☐ A highly visible reminder to grab your hidden "stash kit" from your small fireproof/waterproof safe or other locations with extra keys to your house/vehicle and copies of important personal documents and cash (small bills).

☐ Additional highly visible reminder note to retrieve items

stored elsewhere (e.g. sleeping bags hung in a nearby closet)

☐ Important documents on a USB thumb drive.

☐ PETS: sturdy leash, harness, collar with ID tags; crate for smaller animals if leash not appropriate; collapsible water bowl; minimum 7-day supply of normal food and medications.

APPENDIX C:
GET HOME BAG CHECKLIST

A Get Home Bag is a version of your Go Bag stored at your workplace; its purpose is to assist you to get back home—just one time—without access to your normal means of transportation. Store this backpack at your desk; do not assume you will have access to your vehicle or other areas of your workplace.

☐ Ergonomic small/medium sized backpack.

☐ Water purification bottle, a Nalgene bottle with purification tablets, or a LifeStraw or Sawyer product.

☐ Food: lightweight, nutrient dense food (energy bars).

☐ Ham, FRS, or GMRS two-way radio with instruction manual (store batteries outside of the units themselves).

☐ Two flashlights (one handheld, one headlamp) with extra batteries stored exterior to flashlight.

☐ Small first aid kit, supplemented with Celox, trauma

pads, athletic tape, small bottle of Betadine or other non-allergen antiseptic, and disposable gloves.

☐ Signal whistle.

☐ Lighter or waterproof matches.

☐ P100 masks and additional daily replacement filters; I like the both the 3M 7500 Half Face Piece Respirator and 3M 8293 P100 Disposable Particulate Respirator products.

☐ Backup glasses, contact lenses with solution, hearing aids with batteries.

☐ Sanitation: toilet paper, moist towelettes.

☐ Personal hygiene and comfort items: menstrual products, lip balm, pain relievers.

☐ Pocket multi-tool knife.

☐ Work gloves.

☐ Cell phone battery backup: recharge monthly or per instructions.

☐ Survival sleeping bag or two Heat Sheet blankets and

duct tape to make your own emergency version bag; avoid the ubiquitous and ineffective Mylar blankets.

☐ Tarp with 100' paracord to secure it overhead; second ground tarp.

☐ Sturdy shoes (leave your fancy work shoes at work).

☐ Complete change of sturdy clothing including a long-sleeved shirt and long pants.

☐ Two pairs of hiking socks.

☐ Eye protection: sunglasses, safety goggles, and hat.

☐ Appropriate weather protection: rain poncho or shell jacket, sunscreen, cold weather jacket.

☐ Regional map with reunification location(s) and possible evacuation routes marked.

☐ Notebook and pencil.

☐ Sillcock key to access water from commercial buildings.

☐ Important documents on a USB thumb drive.

APPENDIX D: REUNIFICATION PLAN

A reunification plan is a documented strategy you co-create to gather your loved ones after an emergency incident occurs. Whether the incident is large or small, you'll sleep better and enjoy life more knowing that you have an agreed-upon plan in place.

This plan is best created **before** a disaster strikes when you 1) are thinking clearly and calmly, 2) can make any needed purchases, and 3) can have any required conversations inside or outside of your family circle.

This approach is best looked at through a lens of love, not fear. This is particularly important for younger children and elderly parents.

Loved Ones (people and pets):

☐   _____

☐   _____

☐   _____

☐   _____

APPENDIX D: REUNIFICATION PLAN

Agreements:

☐   Self-care: applying the "rule of threes" (three hours: shelter; three days: water; three weeks: food).

☐   Who stays in place (based on age) and who searches?

☐   Who looks for who first?

☐   Emergency supplies location(s): _____

Out-of-State Contacts (names and phone numbers):

1. _____

2. _____

3. _____

Meeting Spots:

1. Outside of home: _____

2. Outside of neighborhood: _____

3. Outside of region: _____

Local Authorized Guardians (for children):

	Name	Phone	Address
1.			
2.			
3.			
4.			
5.			
6.			
7.			
8.			
9.			
10.			

ABOUT THE AUTHOR

"Resilience is a worthwhile pursuit." – Scott James

BusinessWeek named Scott James as one of "America's Most Promising Social Entrepreneurs" and *Forbes Magazine* profiled him as a "Game Changer."

The products from his companies have been featured in publications as diverse as Oprah's *O Magazine*, *National Geographic*, *Parents Magazine*, the *Washington Post*, *Outside Magazine*, and *US News & World Report*. His media projects range from the opening films at the United Nations Climate Change Summits (Producer Lyn Lear and Director Louie Schwartzberg) to the breakthrough nature-based series on Netflix (title series: "Moving Art").

Scott was awarded the *Governor's Award of Excellence in Service* by the state of Washington for his nonprofit community preparedness work. Scott's training includes permaculture, Transition Towns, CERT, as well as mindful movement techniques such as MovNat, AcroYoga, and vinyasa yoga... all of which tend to be reflected in his work.

Scott previously worked in the high-tech sector, including Visio and Microsoft, and completed degrees at Baylor University and the University of Notre Dame. He lives with his wife and children on an island micro-farm in the Pacific Northwest.

Scott does 1:1 sessions with top performers and small teams of senior thinkers, particularly among the social entrepreneurship tribe. You can learn more at www.scottjames.me.

This is his first book.

ACKNOWLEDGMENTS

No good book about community-building happens without a real live community standing behind it.

In addition to thanking the local heroes I interviewed and our eagle-eyed advance readers (especially Kimberley Gallagher, Leslie Marshall, Walter Sprowls, and Mike Montfort), I'd like to express gratitude to:

- Dr. LuAn Johnson for creating the MYN program.
- BIFD Fire Chief Hank Teran, Fire Marshal Luke Carpenter, and COBI Emergency Management Coordinator Amber Richards. I keep that challenge coin close to me, Chief!
- My parents for putting up with me for the first 18 years of my life, and my in-laws for creating that amazing being known as Susan.
- John Perkins for asking me tough questions.
- The Fandango Brothers for always being there.
- My children, for being my role models.
- And most importantly to Susan: my wife, best friend, and soul mate...the depth of gratitude I have for you is quite literally beyond words.

ADDITIONAL HELP

Over the course of researching and writing this book, I developed a deep network of community leaders, doers, and builders from neighborhoods across the nation. Should you be interested in engaging myself or my team on your project, please visit preparedneighborhoods.com to learn more.

INDEX

CPSIA information can be obtained
at www.ICGtesting.com
Printed in the USA
FSHW01n1550021018
52537FS